A Family's Heartbreak

A Parent's Introduction to Parental Alienation

Michael Jeffries

with

Dr. Joel Davies

A Family's Heartbreak, LLC
Stamford, Connecticut

A Family's Heartbreak, LLC

Suite 202
1250 Summer Street
Stamford, Connecticut

Design and Layout
Inergy Group
Wilton, Connecticut

Library of Congress Catalog Number 2007929695

ISBN 978-0-9796960-1-5

Printed in the United States of America
1st Printing

A Family's Heartbreak
http://www.afamilysheartbreak.com

Dedication

This book is dedicated to my son Adam.

You are in my heart and thoughts and one day, I hope, in my life.

Table of Contents

Introduction

IN THE SPAN OF SEVEN DAYS I filed for divorce, was arrested and falsely accused of child abuse. I also walked into a clinic with all the symptoms of a heart attack. But you know what? Those events were the high points of my week. Divorce, arrests, child abuse charges and heart attacks are like marching in the Disney World parade compared to the world of parental alienation.

The concept of parental alienation is pretty simple – one parent deliberately damages, and in some cases destroys, the previously healthy, loving relationship between his or her child and the child's other parent. In a severe case the alienating parent and child work together to successfully eliminate the previously loved Mom or Dad from the child's life.

My introduction to parental alienation began on the night of July 14, 2004. Until that night my 11-year-old son and I had a wonderful relationship. By the early morning hours of July 15, 2004 we didn't have a relationship.

I know what you're thinking – a normal, healthy father/son relationship doesn't go from hugs to heartbreak in a few hours. I believed the same thing. I was wrong. Parental alienation is like a train barreling through a dark tunnel with its lights off. I was standing in the middle of the tracks when the train emerged from the darkness. I never saw it coming.

Of course, now I can look back and say I should have at least heard the train coming. Now I can point to things my then-wife said to my son one and even two years before that might have set off alarms in my mind. But my son and I had a normal, healthy relationship. I couldn't conceive that any parent would do something so emotionally destructive to his or her child. What I didn't realize is that a variety of emotional issues could combine with the anger, hurt and bitterness of divorce to drive some people to unimaginably vindictive and destructive heights.

On that July night my attorney hadn't even finished drafting my divorce complaint when my future ex-wife started screaming at me within earshot of my son. According to her I was solely responsible for our impending divorce. "Your father is abandoning *us*," she told him.

My ex-wife had my son sleep in her bed that night. He was still sleeping in her bed when I moved out of the house one month later. "I need you to protect me," she kept telling him.

Before I moved out, I couldn't even get him to have dinner with me. "Please don't leave me," Mom begged him. "I don't want to be alone."

I've learned a lot about parental alienation since those first nights. I've had a lot of time on my hands. As I write this, I haven't spent any time alone with my son in almost three years.

One thing I've learned is that an alienating parent is only interested in filling his or her unhealthy emotional needs at the expense of the other parent and their child. The alienating parent doesn't understand that he or she is also hurting the child by forcing the kid to choose a side in the parental conflict.

I've also learned that parental alienation is not just a single crime against the other parent, but three crimes against the child.

The first crime is that the alienating parent doesn't acknowledge that every child is one half of each parent. Every time the alienating parent tells the child how horrible the other parent is, the alienating parent is telling the child that half of him (or her) is horrible.

The second crime is that the alienating parent teaches the child that cutting off contact with people is an acceptable way to handle anger, hurt and disappointment. The world is full of people. One day the child will be an adult. The child will grow up without the appropriate coping skills to have normal, healthy relationships with other adults.

The third crime is that one day the child will look back on the alienating parent's behavior from an adult perspective. He or she will then realize that the alienating parent robbed the child of something very precious – the love and attention of the other parent. The child-turned-adult will realize that the trust placed in the alienating parent was misplaced. He or she will feel betrayed. At that point the adult will not just have one damaged relationship with a parent, but damaged relationships with both parents.

The third crime is the worst crime of all.

I've learned so much about parental alienation I decided to write this book. But before you read any further there's something you should know. I'm not a psychologist. I'm not a lawyer. I'm just a Dad. That's all. A long time ago I would have identified myself as a journalist, but my last byline was during President Ronald Reagan's administration. The statute of limitations on my journalism credentials expired long ago.

Yet my old journalism experience came in handy when I started studying parental alienation. My goal was to regain my relationship with my son. I knew I lived on an emotional roller coaster of anger, depression, helplessness and disillusionment. How were these emotions affecting my ability to achieve my goal? I couldn't imagine what my son was living through. How could I address his issues when I didn't even know what they were? What about family court judges, attorneys, family relation counselors, psychologists, and even the police? How could these divorce-war veterans help, or hurt, my chances of ever having a normal relationship with my son again?

I approached parental alienation like a journalist approaching a news story. I gathered the facts. I interviewed a variety of people – therapists, attorneys and victims. And I passed on everything I learned to the psychologists, attorneys and counselors involved in my case.

Guess what? Many of these professionals had never heard of parental alienation. And the few that had heard of it didn't really understand how to approach a severe case legally or therapeutically. During my crash course in parental alienation I found lots of valuable books on children and divorce. These books discussed alienation-type symptoms, but few books tackled parental alienation head on.

One book that did tackle the subject was Dr. Richard Gardner's *The Parental Alienation Syndrome*. Gardner's book became my bible. I quoted Gardner chapter and verse when I talked to people involved in my case. But Gardner wrote his book for psychologists and attorneys. On the title page of *The Parental Alienation Syndrome*, Gardner even calls his book "a guide for mental health and legal professionals." Naturally, Gardner used a lot of legal and psychological jargon to explain parental alienation.

Since Gardner talked about the life of an alienated parent in clinical terms, I wrote *A Family's Heartbreak: A Parent's Introduction to Parental Alienation* to address alienation in human terms. The book is based on a true story. I wrote it from a parent's perspective. There's a big difference between clinically dissecting the anatomy of an alienated parent and being on the receiving end of the alienating behavior. Think about the difference between studying a driver's manual and climbing behind the wheel of a car for the very first time. Reading the manual doesn't quite measure up to stepping on the gas pedal.

Since I'm not a psychologist, I left the psychological analysis in this book to a professional with experience helping parental alienation families. I shared my story with him. You can sit in on our "sessions" and hear him clinically explain parental alienation. I'll also give you my perspective on parental alienation. I've learned a lot about the legal and psychological professionals forced to deal with this relatively new phenomenon. Perhaps my perspective will save you some time and money. Maybe my experience will help convince legal and mental health professionals that parental alienation is not something they can just dismiss as "bad parenting." Most of all, I hope my experience will help your family avoid what my family went through.

A big part of this book relates examples of alienating behavior. Each one is true. I've presented some of these examples in the form of a journal. This isn't merely a writer's technique. I really kept a journal in the years leading up to and immediately following my divorce. How the journal developed is a story in itself.

At first I told myself I was keeping a journal because I would never remember all the incredible but true events I would need to remember if my divorce went to trial. I was right on both counts. We went to trial, and a large portion of my testimony focused on my future ex-wife's alienating behavior. I wouldn't have remembered a fraction of that behavior without the journal. I highly recommend keeping a journal to anyone who anticipates a nasty trial and child custody battle.

I also discovered that keeping a journal is good therapy. There were many times during my ordeal when I became frustrated or angry. My overwhelming desire at those times was to call someone, anyone, involved in my case and just start yelling. Writing down my frustrations rather than subjecting someone to them was a much better way to handle my emotions.

One day I was writing in my journal when the old journalist inside me re-emerged. I began thinking about parental alienation as a story that needed telling. I found myself editing my journal entries like a copy editor – shortening sentences, comparing verb tenses and double-checking facts. At that point I began not only writing for me but also for you.

Since I was writing for both of us, I had to make some decisions on your behalf. I edited the story heavily to keep the focus on alienation rather than divorce. I also grouped similar examples of alienating behavior together in the journal chapters to illustrate certain concepts better. Finally, I had to make a decision on the use of gender and pronouns when talking about parents and children.

I couldn't write an entire book writing Mom or Dad, him or her, he or she, every time I referred to a parent. In some chapters I thought it was important to remain gender neutral in my references to the alienating parent. Despite my best efforts, you'll notice how awkward the language became. So in other parts of the book I picked a gender for the alienating parent, the alienated parent and the alienated child and stuck with those choices. I also had to decide whether to discuss the alienated child in the singular "child" or the plural "children." So in the pages that follow the alienating parent is generally described as female. The alienated parent is male. The alienated child is male and referred to in the singular rather than the plural.

To be honest, I didn't spend much time considering alternatives. I am an alienated father, I was married to an alienating mother and my son is an alienated child. I tried not to confuse either of us by using one set of pronouns to tell my family's story and another set of pronouns for generic references.

I sincerely apologize to all alienated Moms if I make it appear that only Dads are victims of parental alienation. Fathers successfully alienate children from mothers too. I've heard from many alienated mothers who are suffering the pain and heartache that only an alienated parent can know. I decided to title this book, *A Family's Heartbreak: A Parent's Introduction to Parental Alienation*, because Moms, Dads and children are victims of alienating behavior. In the final analysis, an alienating parent is an alienating parent – regardless of gender. If alienated mothers were to change all my male references to female references and vice versa, the examples and explanations of parental alienation would apply equally to them.

Another decision I had to make was whether to follow Dr. Richard Gardner's lead and write about parental alienation as a syndrome, PAS, or focus on parental alienation behaviors. In this case I did spend a long time considering my decision.

I ultimately decided to drop "Syndrome" from all my parental alienation references because PAS isn't in the DSM -- the psychology profession's Diagnostic and Statistical Manual. The manual is the clinician's bible – a guide to symptoms and syndromes and the definitive diagnosis on any legitimate mental health condition.

PAS may not be in the DSM, but alienating behavior still inflicts pain, heartache and incalculable emotional damage on the children, parents and extended family members involved in these horrible situations. Parents on the receiving end of alienating behavior don't really care if professionals classify the behavior as a syndrome or a bad alignment of the stars and planets. They just want someone to help them restore their previously normal, loving relationships with their children.

I believe one day mental health professionals will classify parental alienation as a "Syndrome." Until then, I am quite comfortable writing about "parental alienation" as behavior and let others debate what to call this very destructive family dynamic. However, I did use the phrase "Parental Alienation Syndrome" or "PAS" in this book when I discussed or quoted other professionals who used the phrase in their work.

I didn't plan on writing the definitive work on parental alienation and in that respect I've succeeded. Writers do their best work writing about their experiences. Not all alienation cases resemble my family's story. An alienated parent needs to examine his or her own personal situation and consult with professionals before completely understanding the circumstances of his or her own case. But whether you are male or female, I hope this story helps you find some answers, comfort and solutions to your alienation nightmare.

I also hope you become outraged that parents alienate their children from the other parent. I hope you become further outraged that judges, attorneys and many mental health professionals consider the actions of an alienating parent just part of a normal day at the office when working divorce and child custody cases. I hope you recognize that parental alienation is a form of emotional child abuse that we can't ignore any longer.

Most of all, I hope that this book, in some small way, helps alienated parents and children begin rebuilding their previously loving relationships.

Mike Jeffries
February 2007

Office of
Dr. Joel Davies

Dr. Davies: Hello Mike. I'm Dr. Davies. Please come in. Have you ever worked with psychologist before?

Mike: No, I never really thought I needed a psychologist before.

Dr. Davies: A psychologist can fill a number of different roles for a patient. It really depends on what the patient wants to get out of the therapy. What are you looking to take away from these sessions?

Mike: I'm looking for information. I want you to educate me about parental alienation.

Dr. Davies: When most people want information they take a class or go to the Internet. Therapy is primarily for people who want to understand themselves better. Is understanding also a goal?

Mike: I guess it is. I need to understand why my wife does what she does, why my son acts the way he acts, and why I feel the way I feel.

Dr. Davies: Okay, that's a start. Why don't you tell me what's going on with you, your wife and your son.

Mike: My wife and I are getting divorced, and she turned my son against me. She didn't want the divorce. She did everything she could to keep me in the marriage. But when she saw I was still leaving, she attacked me where she knew it would hurt the most – my child. I don't know. Maybe she thought if she turned him against me I would stay because I couldn't stand the thought of not seeing him. But I'm not divorcing him. I love him. I want him to live with me half the time. She even turned him against my family. He won't talk to them now either. How can anyone do that to a little boy? And she had me arrested. She said I beat her. I never beat her. She said I physically abused my son. How can she lie like that? Now he even believes I abused him. That's disgusting, I would never...

Dr. Davies: Slow down, I think we better start from the beginning. Let me ask you a few questions.

1

Normalcy

I'M 44 YEARS OLD AND I have these dreams.

I dream my 11-year-old-son is hugging me. I dream he grabs my hand as we walk down a crowded street. I dream he smiles because he is happy to see me. All these dreams end the same way. I start crying because Adam and I are together again. Then I wake up with mixed emotions. I'm grateful for the few seconds of subconscious normalcy, but sad that my dreams are the only place Adam and I have a normal relationship.

Up until recently my life was so normal it was boring. I come from a typical middle class family. Dad owned his own business. Mom stayed home. I'm the oldest of three children. I've got two years on my sister Jill. My brother Steve is the baby of the family. I've got six years on him.

The three of us had a normal childhood. Jill and I only had one fight growing up. Unfortunately for Mom and Dad that fight began in 1962 and lasted until 1978. But Jill and I got along great once I left for college, and we stopped sharing a bathroom, the telephone and oxygen.

Steve and I got along great right from the start. He really looked up to his big brother. In retrospect I probably should have fought more with Steve. Then maybe he wouldn't have followed my career path into journalism. I cost Steve thousands of dollars in lost wages by not going into medicine.

I married my high-school sweetheart straight out of college. She was a nice Jewish girl from my hometown. We were kids when we got married. We were still kids when we got divorced. Thankfully, we didn't have any kids of our own.

I met Beth a year or two after my divorce. At the time I was working in Public Relations during the day and acting in Community Theater at night. One Sunday my friend Matt and I were going to spend the afternoon auditioning for a show. Actually, the audition would only take a couple of minutes. We would spend the rest of the afternoon flirting with good-looking, outgoing actresses and dancers at what is affectionately called a cattle call. I told Matt I would pick him up and drive to the audition. When I arrived at his house and knocked on his door, Beth answered. She was going to paint Matt's den with his wife while the two of us pretended to be actors.

Rumor has it that I took one look at Beth that day and told Matt I was going to marry her. I don't remember saying that. But for almost 20 years everyone repeated the story so many times that if it wasn't true then, it's true now. I consider the story my own personal urban legend.

Beth was married when I met her. That didn't stop us from talking on the phone and seeing each other while her husband worked. Beth was perfect for me. Back then I defined perfect as anyone who was the exact opposite of my first wife. Beth met the requirements. My first wife was short. Beth was tall. My first wife talked a lot. Beth hardly talked at all. My first wife was cute. Beth was gorgeous. My first wife was Jewish. Beth was a non-practicing hybrid of various Christian religions. Beth and I were married in 1987.

Beth wasn't real close to her family. She didn't invite them to our wedding even though they only lived a few minutes away. In fact, her family didn't even meet my family until Jared was born. Jared was planned. The big family meeting wasn't.

My father was standing at the nursery window in the hospital admiring his first grandson. With his chest puffed out and a big smile on his face he turned to the woman next to him and proudly boasted, "That's my grandson in that bassinet." The woman proudly fired back, "That's my grandson too!" The woman was Beth's mother.

Beth was the second of five children. When Beth was little, she supposedly spent time in an orphanage after her mother got sick and her father couldn't take care of her and her brothers. Her father, according to Beth, used to beat her youngest brother. She also told me her parents didn't speak to her for years because Beth's first husband was Jewish. When her father was in his 70s he left Beth's mother. They never divorced. He just moved out of their house. Beth's brothers stopped talking to their father when he moved out. The "boys" were in their 30s, single and living at home at the time.

Beth didn't speak to her sister Mary the entire time we were married. She said Mary was selfish and self-absorbed. I finally met Beth's sister at their mother's funeral. Beth and I had been married more than two years at the time. I watched Mary go through her parent's home after the funeral service and put aside things she wanted to take with her when she left. Beth's description of her sister seemed to fit.

I believed all Beth's stories. Why wouldn't I? What little I saw of Beth's family wasn't very impressive. And Beth was very sweet back then. She would do anything for anyone. She babysat, painted, drove and cooked for anyone who needed help. She took in stray animals. Beth was a walking Toyota commercial – you asked for it, you got it. I often teased Beth that her family was the *Munsters* and she was Cousin Marilyn – the only normal one – even though the rest of her family probably considered Beth the oddball.

Once or twice in the early years of our marriage Beth had problems with women friends. These incidents always ended in a permanent falling out. Beth's once-close girlfriend would disappear from our lives. I never gave these disappearances a lot of thought – even when Beth's stories of petty offenses she suffered at their hands seemed just a little too far fetched. Beth did have girlfriends who endured. I figured Beth could decide for herself which friendships were worth working at and which ones weren't meant to be.

We were married two years when Jared was born. Jared was smart from the day he was born. When he was in kindergarten he became bored with the cute little counting game his teacher had running on the computer. Jared asked his teacher if he could do something else on the computer. The teacher said no. Jared didn't mind. He just changed the password and shut off the computer. No one played that counting game again that day.

Later on Jared was too smart for the third grade. He ended up skipping a year in school but not before having problems with his third grade teacher. For discipline, this teacher made Jared write down all the counties in the state. We lived in Pennsylvania at the time. Pennsylvania is a big state. Jared spent a lot of time writing.

Jared didn't mind rewriting the counties over and over again. He enjoyed the exercise so much he started writing down

4

the counties even when he wasn't in trouble. He always had a fresh copy of counties to hand in to his teacher when he needed one. He also had plenty of copies to sell to his classmates when they were in trouble. When his teacher finally caught on to Jared's entrepreneurial approach to the third grade, she wasn't amused. She didn't give Jared high marks for his understanding of supply-side economics either.

Adam came along in 1993. When Beth was pregnant, people said to me, "You have a boy. I'll bet you want a girl this time, don't you?"

I always answered honestly – no. Jared was four at the time. I liked raising a son, and I was proud of Jared. I figured if we had another boy, I would just use the same parenting skills and get the same results. I was smart enough to know that a little girl would require an entirely different set of parenting skills. I wasn't interested in messing up a successful formula.

Adam put us on notice right from the start that life with him was going to be far different than our life with Jared had been. Jared started sleeping through the night when he was six weeks old. He slept soundly too. The kid slept through Hurricane Andrew; the category-five storm that hit South Florida when Jared was a toddler.

Adam, on the other hand, refused to sleep through the night. As an infant he would cry until I came into his room. Five nights a week I would lie down on the floor beside his crib and pretend to fall asleep. Adam would lie down too. When I thought he was sleeping, I would crawl out of his room. But Adam was pretending too. He would start screaming the minute I got out the door. Finally, I stopped pretending to sleep on the floor and actually started doing it. I don't know if Dr. Spock would have endorsed my solution to the problem, but after too many nights without enough sleep I really didn't care.

As a pre-teenager Adam was still waking up in the middle of the night and looking for someone to stay up with him. I was generally the person Adam looked for. He would walk past Beth's side of the bed, come to my side, wake me up and ask me to lie down with him. We would go back to his room and lie down. I usually fell asleep within seconds. Eventually Adam would wake me up again – this time to tell me I was snoring and I should go back to my own bed.

Naturally, there were other differences between the kids. Jared never really shared my enthusiasm for working out and exercise. Adam did. He would come to the gym with me on the weekends. I taught Adam how to lift weights. We rode exercise bikes and ran on treadmills together. The best part of the morning was our time together after our workout. Adam and I would sit in the gym's snack area munching on muffins and drinking Gatorade. The breakfast of champions, I always told him.

Adam and Jared both enjoyed riding their bicycles with me – and not just the occasional spin around the block. Adam rode 20 miles with me when he was five. When he was ten he joined me and 35,000 other riders in Bike New York, a 42-mile trek through the city's five boroughs. The next year Jared joined us for the ride. Adam gave Jared the benefit of his experience – telling him how far to the next rest stop, pointing out the potential wrong turns. I enjoyed watching Adam show his older brother the ropes.

Adam, Jared and I also shared a passion for science fiction – particularly *Star Trek*. We weren't hard-core Trekkies – running around with pointy ears and plastic phasers – but we did enjoy watching the television shows. Adam and I even read a few of the Trek novels. For me, the best part of *Star Trek* was the conversations I always had with Adam after watching a show or finishing a book.

Adam understood that *Star Trek* wasn't real. Sometimes he just had a hard time understanding that what he was watching didn't have to make a lot of sense. For example, if the Enterprise crew escaped from the space anomaly by emitting a polarized burst with particles from the ship's anti-matter containment field, Adam wanted to know why they just didn't reroute the plasma from the warp core reactors through the deflector shields instead. He always thought his idea would work better and faster. I never argued with Adam's Vulcan-like logic, although I did occasionally point out that faster wasn't necessarily better when you have a full hour of television to fill.

If it sounds as though I had close relationships with my sons, that's because we did have close relationships. The boys and I were close even though I was the family disciplinarian. Our house was the ultimate, "Just wait until your father gets home" house. Even the kids wanted me handling the discipline. Beth's basic approach to discipline was to overreact.

There's no better example of discipline Beth style than what happened one morning outside the gates of Disney World in Orlando, Florida. Jared and Adam got a little wild in the back seat of the car – nothing serious, just typical kid stuff. But Beth wasn't in the mood. She turned around and threatened both boys, "If you don't behave, we're not going to Disney World."

Adam was only five or six at the time. But even he recognized three key flaws in Beth's threat.

First, after driving three hours the night before and staying over in a hotel, we were only one big mouse step away from the Magic Kingdom. Second, Adam saw us purchase our multi-park, multi-day tickets at the hotel just a few minutes before. Third, I was laughing.

But that was Beth. She always threatened cruel and unusual punishments that far exceeded the crimes. And she never followed through on any punishment. If Jared interrupted her when she was on the phone, she would yell, "No video games for a month." Both

Jared and Adam knew Jared would be playing video games faster than you can say, "Nintendo." Even Beth recognized she never followed through. That's why when the boys really stepped out of line she simply said, "Just wait until your father gets home."

In these instances I sometimes yelled at the kids. Other times I talked very softly to them. But my message was always consistent, "You can act any way you want, just know that every action carries consequences." When the kids were little the consequence for bad behavior might be a smack on the bottom. When they got older the consequences tended to focus on early bed times, lost privileges or missed allowances. But no matter what the punishment, I always followed through. And I always ended the discussion with one simple question. I asked, "Was it worth it?" Jared generally admitted the crime was not worth the consequence. Adam rarely, if ever, agreed that behaving would have been a better choice.

I can't say Beth had bad relationships with the boys. She was always close to Adam. He was her baby. But over the years her relationship with Jared deteriorated.

One reason Beth and Jared drifted apart was a teenage boy's natural tendency to identify less with his mother, and more with his father, as he got older. Another reason was Beth's natural non-verbal approach to life. She just wasn't a big talker. When Jared hit his teen years and that shut-down mechanism in every teenage boy's head engaged, limiting his conversation to single syllable responses, you could literally count the words Beth and Jared exchanged during the day. They just never talked much.

But the biggest reason Beth's relationship with Jared deteriorated was because Jared takes after me. Jared talks like me and acts like me. As our marriage fell apart, Beth looked at Jared and saw me. She took her frustrations out on him. And Jared was smart enough to realize what was happening. Jared withdrew further from Beth into his world of school, friends and activities. When Jared needed a parent, he came to me.

Adam, on the other hand, takes after both his parents. Physically, he is all me – bad hair and all. But mentally and emotionally Adam is equal parts Mom and Dad.

From Beth, Adam inherited his love of art, his interest in music and a hatred of losing.

Vince Lombardi, the late coach of the Green Bay Packers, once said, "I never lost a football game. I did, however, occasionally run out of time."

Adam is a Lombardi disciple. He refuses to lose. If Jared is beating him at a video game, Adam turns off the game before it ends. Adam stopped playing organized basketball on a team I coached because he couldn't stand the thought that other kids were better players capable of beating our team. I often believe Adam, the alienated child, thinks our current relationship is some sort of giant game. He's determined to win the game over "his rights" and determined that I lose. Adam has an advantage over Lombardi. He isn't playing with a game clock.

Once upon a time Adam was full of sensitivity, consideration and empathy. He would break into tears if he saw someone crying. When I sprained my ankle before a business trip, it was Adam, not Beth or Jared, who brought me ice, helped me pack and hobble around the house.

One of the great ironies of our current relationship is the child who was so sensitive, considerate and empathetic before being alienated is so insensitive, inconsiderate, and callous towards his previously loved Dad today.

* * * *

9

Dr. Davies: I'm afraid we're out of time for today.

Mike: So what do you think about what I told you?

Dr. Davies: For the most part it sounds like you lived a pretty normal existence. But some things you said were significant red flags that you missed or chose to ignore regarding Beth. Naturally, some of what I'm about to say is conjecture. I wasn't there. But you described a person who wasn't involved with her family of origin and a family that didn't communicate. They got angry. They stayed angry. They didn't resolve anything. They stopped talking to each other. Beth brought these experiences with her when you started a family together. And Beth's experiences continue to play a role in your situation today.

Mike: What role do they play today?

Dr. Davies: One of the most significant points is related to what we call "object relations." Object relations are how you see yourself in relationship to other people and how you define yourself and your place in the world. Based on what you've said, Beth's object relations weren't healthy. They were altered. For example, physical and/or emotional abuse can skew a child's normal, healthy balance between dependence and independence; good self-esteem and poor self-esteem; assertion and passivity. If a child's parents or primary caregivers don't deal with anger appropriately – for example, if the caregivers stop talking to each other, end relationships and never resolve anything – their unhealthy approach to anger resolution affects the child's ability to have healthy relationships with others. The child's ability to trust other people is the biggest casualty of skewed object relations.

Mike: And the child carries these damaged object relations into adulthood and his or her adult relationships?

Dr. Davies: In order for a person to have healthy relationships as an adult it is important that he or she had healthy relationships with others as a child. Children need to know that it's okay to get angry. They need to know that anger doesn't stop someone from loving the person he or she is angry at. In order for children to have healthy adult relationships, they can't grow up believing that anger leads to silence and the end of a relationship. Quite the opposite – in healthy relationships anger leads to communication, an expression of feelings, problem solving and resolution.

Above all else, children want security, permanence and consistency. When confronted with an angry parent, kids need to know that Mom and Dad aren't abandoning them – physically or emotionally – even if Mom and Dad are angry with them. If experience teaches a child that relationships are by their very definition insecure, inconsistent and temporary, there will be a correlation between unhealthy childhood relationships and difficult adult relationships. You mentioned Beth had close girlfriends that would suddenly disappear from her life. People with unhealthy object relations are unable to maintain close, healthy, long-term relationships. Those relationships don't sustain themselves. They take work. At the first sign of a major conflict, the unhealthy adult has trouble coping and seeing beyond the conflict. The adult doesn't

11

communicate, express his or her feelings or work at resolving the problem. So the relationship ends.

Mike: Come on, everyone has close relationships from high school or college that end. What's the difference?

Dr. Davies: There is no correlation between two high school friends drifting apart and an adult who can't maintain a healthy, long-term relationship. The correlation exists between a child who isn't taught how to work through feelings to resolve anger and the adult who doesn't work through feelings to resolve anger. The adult's feelings get stuck in the anger. The person can't move on. He or she will eventually push the anger under the surface – sweep it under the rug – and the anger will come out in other unconscious ways.

Mike: How about me. I was the family disciplinarian. Did assuming those responsibilities lead to my current situation?

Dr. Davies: From what you've said, you modeled consistency. If you said something, that was it. You characterize Beth as over-reacting and never following through. In houses where there are two different parenting styles kids pick up on the inconsistency. Initially, children may find the two styles confusing. But as kids grow older they figure out that if they want something, they go to the parent more likely to give in. Their chances of getting what they want are better. The weaker parent is more likely to give in when the kids start whining and carrying on. This parent doesn't like conflict. This parent wants to be the good guy or the friend rather than the Mom or Dad who says no.

The kids know the stronger parent won't cave. The stronger parent isn't afraid to say no when no is the appropriate response.

Children learn at a very early age that they can get away with certain things with the weaker parent. But even children in healthy two-parent families try and manipulate their situations. They try and cut corners, take the easy way out and put pleasure before work. In healthy families, strong parents set clear boundaries. "No, you must finish your homework before going on the computer." They're not afraid to set boundaries even if the boundaries are unpopular. One parent assuming the disciplinary duties in a family does not necessarily lead to a situation like yours. A situation like yours is the result of many factors. Certainly, a lack of parental consistency could be one contributing factor. We can talk more about that. But more important contributing factors include a parent's fear of abandonment, feelings of emotional incompleteness and dependence and an inability to look at oneself and one's actions objectively. Finally, let's not forget the child. A situation like yours wouldn't exist without a child feeling that he or she must take care of an emotionally weak parent.

But I'm getting ahead of myself. Next time we get together I want to hear more about your marriage.

2

The Foundation

THE STORY BEHIND THE BREAK DOWN of my marriage isn't very interesting. There are lots of unhappy people in unhappy marriages all over the world. These people have the same complaints about their spouses that I had about mine. The courts grant thousand of divorces every year.

The romantics will hate my analogy, but I've often compared marriage to a contract negotiation. In a successful marriage the two married people just keep negotiating the contract details. He compromises on the first point they can't agree on, she compromises on the second point they can't agree on. Maybe they both compromise on point number three. So it goes. Once a decision is reached both people forfeit their initial positions and move on to the next issue – together. The only difference between a successful marriage and a real contract negotiation is that in a real contract negotiation eventually the parties get to sign on the bottom line. No such luck in a successful marriage. The negotiations and compromises continue until death does you part.

Unsuccessful marriages are like contract negotiations too – contract negotiations that fall apart. In these situations the parties do get to sign on the bottom line – the bottom line of their divorce agreement.

I have another theory about marriage. Staying married is easy for two people when every break, lucky bounce, and piece of good fortune comes the happy couple's way. In reality, the true test of a marriage is how the couple handles life's adversity. In the face of adversity, couples with a solid marriage pull together. They face life's challenges side by side and head on. In the face of adversity, couples without a solid marriage pull apart. When the going gets tough, these couples get going – in opposite directions. They pull apart mentally, emotionally and physically.

Beth and I fell into the latter category. Why we fell into that category doesn't really matter. But once we were there we started fighting about all the predictable issues – money, working, family, friends, sex, lifestyle and children. The more we fought, the further apart we drifted. The further apart we drifted, the more we fought. Before too long we were entrenched in our respective positions. She wouldn't negotiate or compromise and neither would I.

Beth and I celebrated our 15th wedding anniversary on October 16, 2003. Actually, celebrated is probably too strong a word. By then Beth and I moved effortlessly and seamlessly from one argument to the next. We never resolved anything. We couldn't even agree on the fact that we never resolved anything.

One argument in particular became a family tradition of sorts. Every year as Thanksgiving approached, Beth and I would argue over how we would spend the holiday. The argument was as predictable as the shoppers who jammed the malls on the day after Thanksgiving.

Growing up a non-observant Jew, Thanksgiving was my favorite holiday. My family didn't really celebrate the Jewish holidays, and we certainly didn't celebrate Christmas or Easter, so Thanksgiving was it. Thanksgiving is still the only holiday my family makes a big deal over. Naturally, I wanted to spend Thanksgiving in Florida with my parents, brother, sister and their families. Once Beth and I drifted apart, she would have rather spent Thanksgiving with terrorists than spend it with my family.

One year Beth agreed to go to Florida for Thanksgiving, and then said she wasn't going. At that point Beth tried convincing Adam to stay home with her. Adam said, "I'm going, and I want you to go." Beth reversed herself again and decided to go. Looking back, this was the first time Beth tried to force Adam to choose between Mom and Dad.

A couple of months later Beth and I were having a heated conversation about our future together. We were both using the "divorce" word frequently at this point. Beth said that if we were divorced she would "turn the kids against me and my Mom." She said she would make the boys hate us.

I didn't understand what my Mom had to do with the argument, and I didn't think much about it at the time. The conversation was heated. People say lots of things they don't mean when they're angry. Surely, I thought, she wouldn't do anything to hurt the kids and their relationships with their Dad and extended family.

It only took me one day to realize I gave Beth too much credit. The next day I made my normal after-school call to Jared and Adam. Nobody picked up the phone. I didn't even reach the answering machine.

Adam later told me that Beth said he shouldn't pick up the phone when I called. I sat both kids down that night and reminded them that I call them every day after school, and they should

17

always answer. From that day forward, Jared or Adam picked up the phone when I called. I didn't give Beth's attempt to disrupt my relationship with the boys another thought. My kids loved me. They knew I loved them. No way could she get between us.

Later that year Beth gave me another preview of things to come. Once again, I was too busy looking past the writing on the wall to read what it said.

My parents were renting a big house in Cape Cod, Massachusetts and treating the entire family to a week at the beach. The whole family would be there – everyone but Beth. She said a week of communal living with my family wasn't her idea of a good time.

Unfortunately, I had to be out of town on business and I would have to miss the first two days of the vacation. My parents said they'd pick up Jared and Adam on the way to the Cape so they could spend a full week at the beach. Beth said no. She would not allow my parents to pick up the kids. "They can wait until you get back," she said. I objected, and nothing was resolved. Beth eventually allowed my sister to drive Jared and Adam to Cape Cod. The kids arrived on time. No real harm was done. At least that was the reason I gave myself for not giving the incident another thought.

Beth's attempts to drive a wedge between the kids and me became less and less subtle. At one point she asked Adam to move back to the old neighborhood in Pennsylvania with her. I didn't understand why Beth wanted to move back to Pennsylvania until much later when she told me she had an affair with a neighbor when we lived there. In any event, I didn't know anything about her plans until Adam asked me why Mom wanted to move back to Pennsylvania if I was staying in New Jersey.

Another time Beth and I had a misunderstanding over the money in our joint checking and savings accounts. Instead of talking to me, she told the kids I emptied out the accounts and wasn't going to support them. When I came home the boys asked me why I wasn't going to support them anymore. I asked them a question back. "Do you really think I wouldn't support you?" They just laughed. Even at 14 and 10 years old, Jared and Adam knew better.

They knew better. That's the main reason I never worried about anything Beth said to the kids. Jared and Adam knew better. I imagined our bond was unshakable, unbreakable and impenetrable.

If anything, I thought Beth was hurting her own relationship with the boys.

Once when Adam asked Beth to take him to the movies, she told Adam he would have to wait until after I got paid – she didn't have any money. Adam called and asked me if Mom really didn't have any money. Whether Beth had enough money for two movie tickets doesn't really matter. Adam didn't trust her to tell him the truth.

Beth also punished Jared and Adam in order to punish me. Like the year we didn't go away for Thanksgiving.

We weren't divorced yet, but I was already treating the holiday as though we were. I had my Thanksgiving with the kids last year. Beth gets her Thanksgiving with the kids this year. I wasn't going to fight Beth over our holiday plans on her year. But Jared and Adam wanted to spend Thanksgiving in Florida. So they fought with her instead of me. At one point, Jared told his Mom, "You never want to go anywhere or do anything that we want to do."

Jared had hit the nail on the head. Beth didn't go anywhere or do anything that we did. Sometimes Beth was absent from the dinner table. She would often pass on our "family" bike rides. Other nights Beth would take off without a word. She wouldn't come home until long after the kids were in bed. I didn't mind. I was happy spending time alone with the boys. My days of being a 24-7 Dad were winding down.

* * * *

Dr. Davies: I'm afraid we need to stop here for today.

Mike: Does parental alienation exist without bad marriages and divorce?

Dr. Davies: It could. However the real correlation exists between parental alienation and parenting. Alienation doesn't exist when there is healthy parenting and co-parenting. But healthy parenting and co-parenting requires teamwork.

The process of parenting should be seamless to children – with both parents sharing similar parenting styles and similar basic philosophies about reward, punishment and consequences. In healthy parenting, both parents have the ability and power to make decisions for the children knowing that the other parent will back him or her up. There is no, "wait until your father gets home," or "wait until your mother gets home." Both parents demonstrate consistency to children – not just consistency as individuals but consistency as a team.

Mike: So what happens when the team breaks up?

Dr. Davies: In a healthy divorce, or uncoupling, parents keep children outside the divorce. The parents recognize that children don't need to hear a lot of details about the marital discord, and they shouldn't be involved in the process. They reassure the children that both parents will continue loving them and being there for them in order to continue meeting their needs. They keep the children out of the domestic squabbles that are a normal part of the separation process so the children don't feel pressured to choose sides.

But parental alienation is all about a child taking either Mom's side or Dad's side. In a parental alienation family one parent typically has dependency and object relation issues. If a woman doesn't have solid object relations, or a solid sense of self, she doesn't see herself as an independent individual. She always sees herself as someone's wife, mother, daughter, sister, etc., and defines herself in terms of how others see her. How she feels about herself depends on how she perceives these other people feel about her. She depends on them to make her feel good. A mother with poor object relations typically depends heavily on the healthy spouse to make her feel good about herself. I'm using "she" generically. Men also have object relation issues.

When the healthy spouse leaves the relationship, the unhealthy spouse's source of support and part of her identity ends. The divorce creates a void that must be filled. Remember, we're talking about a person who can't feel good unless someone assumes responsibility for her emotional health. So the unhealthy parent shifts her dependency/co-dependency needs to the child. The child feels responsible for helping her and making her feel whole again. That responsibility is very unhealthy for the child.

The parent's dependency on the child damages the child's object relations. The child now sees himself based on how well he fulfills his new responsibility. He becomes emotionally dependent on the parent. So you have a very unhealthy situation where the parent is emotionally dependent on the child and vice versa. This unhealthy dependency between parent and child is the foundation of parental alienation.

Mike: Beth always had an unhealthy dependence on Adam. Long before we began talking about divorce she tried convincing him to stay home with her when she didn't want to take a family trip to Florida. Looking back, that was the first time she put Adam in the position of choosing between Mom and Dad.

Dr. Davies: To me, that type of behavior is a red flag identifying the poor boundaries and the dependency issues that are the cornerstone of a parental alienation family. You, Jared and Adam planned on going away and Beth, for whatever reason, didn't want to go. All her insecurity and dependency needs kicked in. She took the very unhealthy step of pulling the child into the decision-making process. Adam, in this case, chose to take the trip. The conflict passed. All four of you moved on – literally and figuratively.

To you, the situation was nothing more than a blip on the screen. You didn't know what you were looking at. However the clinical term for what happened in your family is called splitting. Splitting happens when one person tries turning another person against a third person. Typically, a child tries splitting the parents. The child doesn't like one parent's decision, so he goes to the other parent for support. The child, in effect, tries turning the parents against each other. One parent's turning a child against the other parent is another form of splitting. The child may initially resist, like Adam did, but he still gets the message.

Mike: What message?

Dr. Davies: A child in this position gets to pass judgment on his parents! In his mind, he has the power to say, "One parent is right and the other one is wrong. One parent is good and the other one is bad." Unfortunately, a split child's sense of security – his sense that both parents are qualified to meet his needs and take care of him – gets lost when he starts passing judgment. And the parent who pulled the child into the decision-making process reinforces the concept that one parent, the other parent, is unqualified to take care of the child.

Compare this situation to a healthy family. In a healthy family neither parent abdicates the parental authority. Neither parent gives a young child decision-making power. Naturally, as the child gets older, healthy parents may *involve* him in some decisions. Healthy parents may ask an older child where he would like to spend a vacation. But once an older child voices an opinion the parents reach the decision independently. Then they inform the child what they've decided. The clear boundaries between the child and parents stay in place. The child feels secure, taken care of, and protected.

In an alienated family, or a future alienated family, the child doesn't have these feelings. The child feels vulnerable, confused and internally conflicted. He can challenge parental authority and break down boundaries. In an alienated family, the parent with the damaged object relations elevates the child's status. The child becomes part of the parental dyad and aligns himself with the dependent parent – fulfilling her needs and creating a supportive and dependent bond between the two. At this point, there are no boundaries between the parents and the child. The healthy parent's power is undermined. For a child, this power and the ability to make decisions is intoxicating. If the healthy parent tries breaking this dependent bond and taking back some parental authority, the bond between the child and the dependent parent grows stronger.

Mike: Does a parent with damaged object relations do this to a child on purpose?

Dr. Davies: We're not talking about consciously motivated actions. I look at healthy parents as being logical. If I were to say to a parent, "I think your actions may be harming your child," I believe a healthy parent would stop what he or she is doing and look for ways to change or undo the damage. An unhealthy parent, a parent with damaged object relations, is unconsciously motivated. For reasons that have nothing to do with the child, the parent's motivation is based on getting whoever is closest to fill the void created by the loss of the other spouse. Remember, this is a person with deep-seated dependency and loss issues. When the spouse leaves, she becomes symptomatic. In her mind, her emotions and feelings validate her behavior. She then further justifies her behavior by telling herself that her actions are in the child's best interests – thus elevating her own status as the best kind of parent.

Mike: Besides the exhilaration of the power trip, what is the child thinking when he becomes part of the unhealthy relationship?

Dr. Davies: In a clinical sense, the child becomes emotionally brainwashed. The parent makes the child so dependent on her for his needs; the child feels a big responsibility to take care of the parent. The child is confused. He sees the parent with the damaged object relations suffering. The spouse has abandoned her. The child is in a double bind – he has feelings for the other parent, but he can't express those feelings. He needs to side with the poor, suffering dependent mother. If he sided with the father, in his mind he would be abandoning the mother too.

Mike: So every time Beth put Adam in the middle, gave him this elevated status, I shouldn't have been so casual about it just because Adam made the right decision. Is that what you're saying?

Dr. Davies: Hindsight is 20/20. Without being able to recognize the larger pattern, I wouldn't expect a healthy parent to act any differently than you did. You couldn't see the forest through the trees.

When I treat entire families, I'm detached enough to see the pattern, recognize the big picture and then address the unhealthy behavior within the larger context. But when a person is part of a family, an incident occurs, and it's over quickly. That person won't typically make a big deal out of it because he or she doesn't see, or doesn't want to see, the bigger pattern.

Mike: What do you mean by "doesn't want to see the bigger pattern?"

Dr. Davies: Let me ask you something first. When Beth was angry with you, how did she act?

Mike: When Beth was angry she wouldn't talk to me for days. On the third or fourth day, I would come home from work, and Beth would act like nothing ever happened. Despite the fact that whatever made Beth angry in the first place wasn't resolved, I was supposed to act like nothing happened too.

Dr. Davies: Did you act like nothing happened?

Mike: For years I tried talking to her when she acted that way. I tried resolving whatever caused the silent treatment in the first place. But I could never get her to discuss anything. The process was exhausting. I put all sorts of energy into resolving conflicts that Beth refused to resolve. I learned to just wait for her to get over her anger.

Dr. Davies: Yes, but you also learned your life was easier if you waited for Beth to come around. For a long time you weren't interested in connecting the dots among these isolated incidents, creating the big picture, and discovering that your marriage was infinitely more challenging than you already knew it was. That process would really have exhausted you. You had to reach a point where too many things about your marriage were unacceptable to you before you were ready to connect the dots and deal with the big picture.

Mike: So I contributed to my current situation.

Dr. Davies: What's that old saying? If you're not part of the solution you're part of the problem? But don't be too hard on yourself. I wouldn't expect anyone at this stage of the game to know what is waiting around the corner. A person in your position just tries to manage his or her marriage and family on a day-to-day basis.

3

The Blame Game

YOU KNOW WHAT PARENTAL ALIENATION reminds me of? Parental alienation reminds me of an old-fashioned western.

The good guy wears a white hat and throws his coat over the mud so the lady doesn't get her shoes dirty walking across the street. The bad guy wears a black hat and snarls a lot. The good guy is truthful and honest. The bad guy is a lying cheat. The good guy leaves with the girl. The bad guy leaves in a box.

At least that's the alienating parent's perspective. The alienating parent needs clear-cut good guys and bad guys in order to alienate the child from the previously loved spouse. In this scenario the alienating parent and anyone who supports the alienating position are the truthful, honest, white-hat-wearing good guys. The alienated parent is the lying, cheating, and black-hat-wearing bad guy.

Alienating parents need this good vs. evil battle in order to justify their actions. They must convince the child the other parent is unworthy of the child's love, respect and attention. They must convince attorneys, counselors and even friends that they, not the other parent, are acting in the child's best interests. Finally, they must convince themselves that their alienating behavior is not motivated by anger, hurt and a need for revenge.

Ever hear of the KISS theory? Keep it simple stupid. Alienating parents combine the good vs. evil scenario with the KISS theory and approach the child with very simple, easy to understand concepts. "Dad's the bad guy. He abandoned us. I'm the good guy. I'm not going anywhere." The words may change depending on a couple's situation, but the alienating concept remains the same – everything is the other parent's fault. The family is breaking up and the other parent is to blame. If alienating parents understand their roles in the breakup of families, they certainly won't admit it to anyone – especially to the children they're alienating.

As Beth and I moved closer to the inevitable, Beth wouldn't take any responsibility for the breakdown of our marriage. She wouldn't do anything about it either.

Beth wouldn't go see a marriage counselor. She wouldn't go see an attorney. Beth wouldn't compromise on any of our differences. We reached the point where Beth wouldn't even discuss our differences. The blame, and the responsibility for moving forward, was squarely on my shoulders. The breaking point came in March 2004.

Beth accused me of "playing games" with my annual bonus check. I hadn't received the check yet, but Beth thought I had. She accused me of hiding the check, keeping it from her. Beth's paranoia over the bonus check was her third financial crisis in less than a week. She also questioned one of my ATM withdrawals and accused me of entering a lower payroll deposit amount into our joint checkbook.

Beth said she would hire an attorney to find out what "I did" with the check. We all have our breaking points and that one was mine. I suggested she hire an attorney to represent her during her divorce. I'm filing for divorce, I said, and I'm not turning back.

When Beth saw I was serious, she decided she didn't want a divorce. All of a sudden, Beth was ready for marriage counseling. She was ready to join the family on vacations. She was ready to do anything she could to save her marriage. Beth even tried convincing me she had been acting for ten years – pretending she didn't love or respect me because she was always mad about something I did or didn't do. She wanted a chance to show me "the real Beth."

My wife was good. She almost had me convinced until she came to me one day and asked me to take her bowling. I love to bowl, and in 16 years I was able to get Beth on a bowling alley exactly once. Beth hated bowling. She reminded me she hated bowling every time I asked her to go. Now, all of a sudden, she was ready to hit the lanes. Something stank of insincerity and manipulation. That something was Beth.

Beth continued playing the victim. I was the one with the community theater experience, but Beth was the one earning an Academy Award for her performance as the victim in the Best Dramatic Actress category. And she made sure Jared and Adam had a front row seat for every performance.

Jared and Adam watched her cry. They saw her lose a lot of weight. They saw her pass out – allegedly from stress and depression. They overheard Beth pour her heart out over the phone to her friends. Beth sent the kids a clear message – she didn't want the divorce, I did. She was willing to work out our problems, I wasn't.

My sensitive son Adam rushed to his mother's defense. Adam blamed me for Beth's emotional state. He refused to talk to me for two weeks. Finally, Beth convinced Adam to talk to me. Unfortunately, I believe she brought Adam around by giving him the impression that his parents were working out their problems.

Beth sent me a clear message too. She wasn't really serious about working out our problems. She was only serious about maintaining the status quo. Of course, if in the process of maintaining the status quo, she could improve it in her favor that was even better.

I was still living in the house. I hadn't found an apartment yet. Beth came to me one day and said her therapist wanted to know if I would be willing to do more housework. Supposedly the therapist was concerned about Beth's weight loss and she wanted Beth to take it easy. I said "sure." I was concerned about Beth's weight loss too. But then I asked Beth if she was going to quit her part-time job. She said no. I asked if she was going to stop exercising and working out. She said no again. I asked Beth if she was going to eat more. She said no a third time. I finally asked the obvious rhetorical question. "So the result of this conversation is you are not changing any of your behavior at all to address your weight loss but I'm doing more housework?" Beth couldn't answer me. But the answer was obvious.

Beth wasn't going to change any of her behavior. She just wanted to stay married. The fact that she was married to me fell into the "convenient" category.

Perhaps Beth thought I would change my mind about leaving if she raised the stakes high enough. At one point she said she'd kill herself if I left. She even told me how she planned on taking her life. "I'll take three of my anti-depressants and drink two glasses of wine," she said. Clearly my ex-wife didn't take any pharmacology classes in college.

When Beth saw I was still leaving despite her suicide threat, she was ready to fire the last bullet in her gun. The date was July 13, 2004.

The kids were away – Adam was at Boy Scout camp, and Jared was in Florida. It was the perfect opportunity for me to tell Beth I had found an apartment and was moving out September 1. But she beat me to the punch. "When were you going to tell me you're moving out September 1, she asked?" I swallowed hard. She already knew. "Yea, I'm moving out and filing for divorce," I stammered.

It's funny what people worry about sometimes. Okay, it's funny what I worry about sometimes. I was closing the door on a 16-year marriage and turning my children's lives upside down. But at that particular moment I was primarily concerned with not ruining Jared and Adam's summer vacation. I suggested to Beth that we not say anything to the kids until the week before I was to move out.

I should have known better than to expect Beth to agree with me about anything – especially at this point. Beth said she'd tell the kids "everything" when they come home from their trips. "They won't want any part of you," she said. "Go for it," was the best I could do in response.

On the big-time comeback meter, my retort barely registered. Any fantasies I had that Beth would work with me to put Jared's and Adam's best interests first ended that night.

* * * *

Mike: Did you like my western analogy?

Dr. Davies: Parental alienation often looks like a simple
                             case of good guys vs. bad guys. But there's more to

parental alienation than one parent playing the "good parent" and painting the other parent as the "bad parent."

A key factor that is characteristic in all parental alienation families is the alienating parent's real or perceived fear of abandonment. If the alienating parent is female, somewhere in her past she felt abandoned physically or emotionally by her father or other paternal figure. These feelings are the basis for her fear of abandonment as an adult. Alienating fathers also suffer from feelings of abandonment. For men, the feelings stem from the real or perceived, physical or emotional abandonment by their mothers or other maternal figures.

Mike: Emotional abandonment?

Dr. Davies: One form of abandonment is physical abandonment. In physical abandonment the parent leaves or is physically unavailable. A father who works constantly and is never available to his children is an example of someone who stays in the house but is physically unavailable.

However another form of abandonment is emotional abandonment. A parent who emotionally abandons a child may still live in the house but be cold, unresponsive and emotionally unavailable to the child. An alcoholic parent or a parent suffering from emotional problems could possibly be emotionally unavailable to his children. If a parent leaves the family and is totally unavailable to the child, the child may feel both physically and emotionally abandoned.

Remember when we talked about a child's object relations? The child learns who he is in relation to other people. In real or perceived emotional abandonment, the child believes the parent doesn't care about him and doesn't want to be involved in his life. If he were important, the child rationalizes; the parent wouldn't be cold, unresponsive and emotionally unavailable. Usually the child will internalize or personalize his feelings. "This is about me," the child tells himself, "I must not be good enough. "

A divorce brings these old abandonment issues front and center. As the emotionally healthy parent goes through the process of disengaging from the relationship and moving closer to divorce, the parent with the unresolved abandonment issues experiences those issues all over again. This emotionally unhealthy parent needs someone to take care of her emotionally, someone to fill the void. Since the healthy parent is no longer filling the role, the alienating parent turns to the child.

Mike: So at the end Beth was willing to do anything just so she wouldn't feel abandoned?

Dr. Davies: When Beth realized the divorce was real she started bargaining. You saw a Beth you never saw before. She was willing to reshape herself. She'd go to counseling, go on family vacations and even go bowling. Beth was desperately trying to avoid the uncomfortable feelings and fears that she experienced in the past and never resolved. It was déjà vu all over again. She would have done anything to keep from feeling abandoned.

This is parental alienation "ground zero." Parental alienation is the very negative by-product of how an adult deals with the perceived abandonment. When the abandonment fears become real, the alienating parent will do whatever it takes to regain control and balance in her life. She'll do anything to avoid abandonment – even take her child emotionally hostage.

In Beth's mind, you abandoned her. She needed to make you the bad guy, and she needed Adam to support her position. Beth needed Adam to fill the emptiness. So she told him, "I will never leave you. I won't abandon you. I'm the good parent. Dad's is leaving. He is abandoning us. He is the bad parent."

Mike: So I was right – she presented everything to Adam in simple, black and white, easy-to-understand concepts.

Dr. Davies: The alienating parent has one way of looking at the world. Her world is right vs. wrong, good vs. bad, black vs. white. She tells the child factual things that may or may not be true – Dad stole our money, Dad had an affair, Dad beat me – and leaves out all the gray area that is typically part of any conflict. She also leaves out anything that may indicate that she played a role or had some responsibility for the breakdown of the marriage.

A pre-adolescent child is more susceptible to an alienating parent's "facts" and her black vs. white world because he hasn't begun to think in abstract terms. The child doesn't question authority. A pre-adolescent child thinks concretely and needs his life consistent and secure in order to avoid feeling anxious or scared.

An adolescent child thinks more abstractly and questions authority. He can tell you what two different concepts have in common. As the child gets older he can take the facts, think about them, challenge them and draw his own conclusions.

Mike: Where does the truth enter into this?

Dr. Davies: Whether or not a parent is telling the truth is irrelevant to the child's perception of the truth.

If Beth said there was no money, Adam the pre-adolescent knew you worked and she didn't. If Beth said you were abandoning them, Adam knew you were leaving. Beth's statements became Adam's truths.

Mike: So what does the pre-adolescent child do with this information?

Dr. Davies: The child becomes confused, anxious and sometimes depressed. He sees the parent as the victim and he wants to take care of the parent. Emotionally speaking, you see the child take on much more than he should take on – worrying about the parent, being clingy, compliant and making sure the parent is okay. The parent, who has all the unresolved abandonment issues in her past, now has someone to help keep those feelings away.

This "parent as the victim" scenario is a recreation of the parent's childhood abandonment issues. The parent saw herself as a victim when she was a child, and now she sees herself as a victim as the adult. More important, playing the victim absolves her from taking any responsibility for the situation.

Mike: Is the parent conscious of her behavior and its effect on the child?

Dr. Davies: When an alienating parent is playing the victim, she is falling into an old, very familiar role. She is reacting to very painful emotions and trying to avoid them.

The alienating behavior is conscious. She knows she is saying negative things about the other parent. But she doesn't stop to think about what motivates her behavior. Nor is she conscious of the effect her behavior has on the child. The only thing she knows for sure is that all these old fears from childhood are coming back, and they feel bad to her.

An alienating parent doesn't have a level of consciousness or emotional distance to say, "I can't believe I'm doing this." The parent is ruled by her emotions and unconscious motivation. She is satisfying an emotional need. An alienating parent would have to take a giant step backwards to see her pattern from a logical or less emotional vantage point, and an alienating parent can't take that step.

Mike: So what does she see from her vantage point?

Dr. Davies: Think about your biggest fear that you would do anything to avoid but still must deal with. The steps people take to avoid dealing with these fears are incredible. In order to mitigate the abandonment fears, an alienating parent brings the child into a role designed to make her feel better.

When the abandonment becomes real, her worst fear is realized. At that point her fear turns to anger. There is a mental switch that takes the alienating parent from having her emotional needs met to needing revenge, retribution and payback. I imagine Beth became very angry when she identified a point of no return.

Mike: That's an understatement. Beth's point of no return was July 14th. That mental switch not only was thrown but also got stuck in the anger, revenge and retribution position.

Dr. Davies: An alienating parent at this point is so angry she doesn't realize she is harming the child. We're talking about emotions and unconscious motivations. Emotional people don't always realize what they're doing when they act out of emotion. Most healthy people come down from the anger and think clearly and logically. But remember, an alienating parent's object relations are damaged. In Beth's family people stopped talking to each other when they got angry. They left – if not physically, then emotionally. They never resolved their anger. They may have suppressed the anger and started talking to each other again, but they never resolved the anger.

Next time we get together I want you to tell me what happened on July 14th.

4

Heartbreak

WITH ALL DUE RESPECT to the men and women at Pearl Harbor on that fateful morning in December 1941, July 14, 2004 is my own personal, "day that will live in infamy."

The day began with a long drive to Adam's Boy Scout camp. Beth and I both drove up – separately – to bring Adam home. She got there first and was sitting at one end of the campsite when I arrived. I sat at the other end of the campsite. I'm not sure how many acres the Boy Scouts occupied in Northwestern New Jersey; all I know is the camp wasn't big enough for both of us. I couldn't have cut the tension with a knife – no matter how many Boy Scout badges I might have earned for completing the task.

If Adam was aware that his parent's weren't talking to each other or even sitting together, he didn't show it. He squeezed in every last second of running around with the other scouts – doing his best to ignore his parents' presence and his squad leader's pleas to clean up the campsite. After the parents cleaned up the camp, packed up the gear, and attended the required too-long awards ceremony, it was time to leave. Adam drove home with Beth.

Once we got home I told Beth she should take Adam out to dinner, and I would take him out tomorrow night. Jared wasn't coming home from Florida for another few days. But Beth had Adam invite me to dinner and a movie with them. Unbelievable! I told Adam to go with Mom and come with me tomorrow night. He didn't like it but said okay.

I did things around the house all day – doing my best to stay busy and avoid Beth. She wasn't hard to avoid. Beth spent most of the day in her room whispering into the phone. I didn't care whom she talked to or what she said. Okay, that's not entirely true. I started caring when I heard Beth telling my brother, Steve, her version of why we're getting divorced. As a public service, she also told him what his brother "is *really* like." Most of what she said wasn't true. But if Beth wanted to get under my skin she succeeded. When Beth handed the phone to Adam, I told her if she continued telling my family one lie after another, I'd make sure they never talked to her again. She'd been threatening to come between the kids and me for a year and a half. Two can play that game right?

Wrong. Big mistake. Beth screamed that if I cut her off from my family, she would cut the kids, especially Adam, off from them. And me.

Then for good measure Beth screamed about every slight, every indignity, real or imagined, from our entire 16-year marriage. The line between fact and fiction disappeared. Adam was talking to Steve and Jared from the next room. He shut his door so he wouldn't have to hear his Mom's screaming. But Beth was determined, and loud. She wanted Adam to hear everything. Nothing was too personal or inappropriate for an 11-year-old boy. She wanted Adam to hate me. And she was just warming up.

I heard Adam crying so I went into his room. I was too late. He blamed me for the divorce. Beth obviously had talked to him without me. When I tried calming Adam down, Beth threw more fuel on the fire. She physically got between Adam and me and wouldn't let me near him. Beth threatened to call the police if I touched Adam.

Beth told Adam to come sleep with her in her bed. In the blink of an eye my life had become a grotesque circus worthy of *The Jerry Springer Show*. I imagined the promo. *"Next on Jerry Springer, Mom pulls son into bed to keep Dad away."*

Once in bed, Beth and Adam huddled together as if they needed each other's body heat to stay warm. I stood near the foot of the bed. Beth called me every name she could think of – liar, abuser, cheater, loser, trash, and bastard – and encouraged Adam to repeat everything she said. He did. When I told Adam not to talk to me that way Beth countered and said Adam could talk to me any way he wanted. Adam didn't have to listen to me, she said. He didn't ever have to talk to me again.

I told Adam over and over I loved him and that we'd work things out. Beth shouted over me – one filthy name after another. Every time I moved closer to Adam she threatened to call the police if I touched him.

Beth was doing a great job of destroying me in front of Adam. The only problem was she was also destroying Adam. The kid was torn beyond belief. The pain was etched on his face. At one point, I asked Beth to at least tell Adam that I was a good father. She refused.

I felt like I was driving past a gruesome car wreck – the kind of wreck where your head reflexively turns away because your brain can't process what your eyes would see. My brain couldn't comprehend what I was living through. I finally left the house. I wasn't getting anywhere with Adam. We both needed to calm down.

I drove aimlessly for a while. When I got home I went to my bedroom and pulled down a shoebox from the top of the closet. The shoebox was full of holiday cards from Beth. I had 16 years worth of birthday, anniversary and Valentine Day cards saved in that box and I ripped up each one. Every time I came across a Father's Day card where Beth wrote about what a wonderful father I was, I became even more upset. I couldn't believe the person who wrote those Father's Day notes would go to the lengths Beth went to earlier in order to destroy my relationship with my son. The more cards I ripped up the more upset I became.

Adam heard me and came to see what I was doing. I thought that was a good sign.

When my sensitive son saw me crying he started crying too. I told him I loved him, and I would always love him. I told him we would get through this together. He asked if that meant Mom too. I said no.

Adam kept asking me to try marriage counseling once – just once – and if I didn't like it, I wouldn't have to go again. I explained that marriage counseling didn't work that way. Marriage counseling is a long process that both people have to commit to; both people have to want to make the marriage work. I told Adam my marriage to Mom was too far gone to make that commitment. You can't go just once.

I'm not sure if Adam understood everything I said. But I do know that saying no to Adam was the hardest thing I ever did in my life. I rarely said no to Jared or Adam if they asked for something reasonable, and I knew it was important to them. Tonight Adam asked me to preserve the world he loved. This was the most important request of his young life. And I said no. I caused my son immeasurable pain. I've never felt worse. The

44

desperation on his 11-year-old-face is seared into my brain. The memory will haunt me forever.

Beth barged into the room many times while Adam and I talked. Each time I asked her to go away. Each time she refused. Finally I told Adam that I wouldn't talk to him with Mom present. If she wouldn't leave, I wanted him to go with her and go to sleep. Adam kept asking Beth to leave. She continued standing outside the door listening to every word. She barged in every time I said something she didn't like. We repeated this scene over and over again.

In between Beth's interruptions I talked to Adam about a lot of things – marriage, trust and relationships. I'm sure some of it was over his head. But my messages to him were fairly consistent:

- I loved him, and I would always love him. I knew he loved me. We would get through this together.

- My marriage to Mom was over. There was no trust or respect between us. Despite what Mom continued saying about marriage counseling, marriage counseling could never fix our marriage.

- I'm not perfect. I've made mistakes. I'm human. But I know I'm a good Dad.

- I hadn't loved Mom the way a husband should love his wife for many years. I stayed married to Mom because of him and Jared.

- The reasons for the divorce have nothing to do with him.

- No one else broke up Mom and Dad's marriage. Mom and Dad equally share the blame for the breakdown of the marriage.

- There are two sides to every story, and the truth is usually somewhere in the middle. Finding that middle ground isn't his job. He deserves to have a good relationship with Mom. He deserves to have a good relationship with me.

Beth barged in again sometime around 3:00 a.m. This time I didn't bother asking her to leave. Adam and I had covered enough ground for one night. I told Adam to go to bed. I was emotionally drained. I can't imagine how Adam felt.

* * * *

Dr. Davies: That was a rough night.

Mike: Worst night of my life. Was it inevitable?

Dr. Davies: What you described was the climax of a situation that was predetermined long before it happened. Once a person disengages and removes himself from a spouse with poor object relations, separation anxiety and unresolved abandonment issues, the abandoned spouse's reaction is inevitable. The only surprises are when will it occur and how bad will it be.

What you saw was an adult coming face-to-face with her darkest demons. You saw total panic, anxiety and a loss of control. Lots of people with abandonment issues address those issues long before middle age. But you saw a 40-year-old woman who had never dealt with her unresolved issues. She was falling and trying to regain her balance any way she could.

Mike: So Beth looked to Adam for balance?

Dr. Davies: Yes and no. A person in Beth's situation looks for anyone at that point. She wasn't consciously looking for Adam to save her and make her feel better. He was accessible, available and a willing participant. You were leaving. Jared was emotionally detached from Beth. Adam was the closest one to Beth who had not betrayed or abandoned her, and she was going to make sure it stayed that way. Adam saw her fears and did everything he could do to take care of her.

Mike: Adam was torn apart. I've never seen so much pain on one child's face.

Dr. Davies: It makes me sad to think what goes on in an 11-year-old head at a time like that. A child is typically dealing with his own issues of loss and abandonment. His security, comfort and stability are being ripped away. This is a time when the child needs both parents' reassurance. The child needs to hear that both parents will continue loving him and taking care of him. Your child didn't get that reassurance. Instead, one parent sent the message that the child needed to take care of her. The abandoned parent may threaten to hurt or kill herself if the child doesn't side with her. Sometimes the comments are subtle like, "If you ever leave me, I will die." This type of parent literally burdens the child with her lifetime of betrayal and abandonment issues. What choice does a child have in a situation like that? Either he sides with Mom against Dad, or something bad will happen to Mom. The child feels that he has no choice.

Mike: Was this night one of those defining moments that will affect Adam for the rest of his life?

47

Dr. Davies: Sadly, it will be a very defining moment in his life. The child will carry this burden until someone intervenes so the child can emotionally step aside and stop taking care of his mother. But at this point the parent is holding on to the child for dear life and the child is holding on to the parent for dear life. That bond won't be broken easily.

This unhealthy bond between the parent and child may be characteristic of a variety of clinical issues including enmeshment, dependency and/or a Borderline Personality Disorder. Borderline Personality Disorder is a cluster of symptoms that indicates a person has extremely poor boundaries and a pervasive pattern of instability in interpersonal relationships. A person suffering from Borderline Personality Disorder also is emotionally unstable and suffers from a poor self-image.

You saw Beth become very symptomatic when your desire to leave the marriage became real for her. Consistent with Borderline Personality Disorder, you saw profound changes in her behavior, emotions and thought processes as the impending rejection and loss became apparent. As the abandonment fears became real, you saw an increase in Beth's inappropriate anger. This was her way of dealing with her fear of being alone. People who fear abandonment equate being alone with being bad. If I were a good person, he or she rationalizes, this other person would want to be with me. A person will go to great lengths to dispel this negative thought, even take his or her own child as an emotional hostage.

Mike: What do professionals focus on when working with Borderline Personality Disorder patients?

Dr. Davies: Borderline Personality Disorder is one of the more difficult disorders to treat because symptoms will change without any identifiable rhyme or reason.

People with this disorder display chronic instability beginning in early adulthood. Chronic instability is very common in Borderline Personality Disorder. At one end of the spectrum Borderline Personality Disorder is characterized by feeling out of control, impulsiveness and serious emotional instability. At the other end of the spectrum the patient feels fine. Treating Borderline Personality Disorder patients in their 20s and 30s can be a full-time job for a psychologist. The goals are to help them be more objective in their perceptions, create stable careers and relationships, and make objective life choices. Often as people with Borderline Personality Disorder get older many of their symptoms diminish because they create greater stability in their lives.

Now let's talk about you. How did you feel that night? What was going through your mind?

Mike: My two biggest emotions that night were disbelief and numbness over the loss of control. I lived through it, and I still can't believe it happened. And since I'm a person who is generally in control, the total loss of control was really overwhelming for me.

Dr. Davies: You were like the captain of a ship standing on the shore watching his beloved ship sink into the darkness. You were helpless watching everything you worked for disappear. You couldn't do anything to save it. You had no power or control. You were forced to watch your world, and how you envisioned your world with your son after the divorce, crumble before your eyes. There was absolutely nothing you could have done about it.

Mike: So how would you advise someone to handle a situation like that?

Dr. Davies: The situation you described is not a situation that can be handled or managed. The alienated parent is powerless. The alienating parent is acting illogically. The child is caught in an emotional bind. Everyone's emotions are running high.

This is a situation that could have easily escalated. When emotions run that high there could have been physical violence, and the police would have shown up. Then you would have had a hysterical female on one side, a traumatized child in the middle, and a distraught father on the other side trying to break a strong, unhealthy emotional bond between the mother and child. The officer would have seen the mother and child holding on to each other for support, comfort and safety. Who do you think that officer would have empathized with? The father wouldn't have stood a chance.

All the alienated parent can do is reinforce positive messages – "I love you. I'm still your mother/father. I will always be here for you." He or she should try and remain calm. He or she shouldn't raise his or her voice or use force.

There is a tendency for someone in this situation to try and set boundaries with the alienating parent. But anyone who tries to set clear boundaries with a person who has no boundaries might as well be spitting into the wind. So I dissuade the alienated parent from engaging the alienating parent in conversation with the child present. He or she is not going to win.

Mike: What can a psychologist do for an alienated parent in this situation?

Dr. Davies: Psychologists offer a lot of support and do a lot of hand holding with alienated parents. Parental alienation is something that nobody is prepared for. Most parents have little to no insight into what's about to come. Parental alienation is a very long process of heartache, gaining balance, and being thrown off balance again.

Above all, an alienated parent needs to keep his emotions in check. He needs to learn coping skills and how to get through the alienation one day at a time. He may have other children that still need and depend on him. He probably has a job and responsibilities at work. An alienated parent has to stay strong and emotionally intact to make it through this process.

Mike: How long does the process take?

Dr. Davies: If I answered that question honestly you wouldn't believe me. Let's just say the process takes longer than you're ready to recognize at this point. If I gave you a more specific answer, I'd be the one spitting into the wind. Your "day that will live in infamy" comment was very appropriate.

51

December 7, 1941 was the first day of a long, bitter, painful war. July14, 2004 was the first day of a different kind of war for you.

5

Bad to Worse in 30 Days

July 15

ADAM SLEPT IN THE BED I used to share with Beth last night –
sleeping on what Beth and I used to consider "her" side of the bed
while she slept on "my" side of the bed. He woke up about 12:30
this afternoon and came into my room. I took that as another
positive sign. My optimism was short lived.

When I asked him to go to dinner with me, he asked if
Mom could come. I said no. Adam didn't say anything and left the
room. I ran a few errands and when I came home later in the
afternoon, Beth and Adam were gone. Adam called around 6:00
p.m. to say he was having dinner with Mom.

Close to midnight I found Adam in bed with Beth again. I
went in and kissed Adam good night. Beth told me to get out of her
room. I ignored her. I asked Adam to sleep in his bed. He said he

wanted to sleep with Mom. I asked Adam to have dinner with me tomorrow night. He said if Mom couldn't go, he wasn't going.

Then Beth got into the act. She said Adam didn't have to do anything that he didn't want to do. I continued ignoring her, and that just made her mad. She ordered me out of the room. A quick kiss to Adam's forehead and I was out of there.

Adam was more hardened towards me. He didn't want me kissing him goodnight. He didn't want to hug me. But I guess I couldn't expect too much after he spent all day alone with Beth.

July 16

I asked Adam to go to dinner with me again. He said he wouldn't go to dinner or do anything with me after dinner unless Beth was present.

The day ended with Adam in Beth's bed again.

July 17

The night started out positive enough. Adam came into my room to talk to me. Ever the optimist, I took that as another good sign. But within minutes Adam became rude. Then he decided to leave. I told him to sit down. I wasn't done talking.

In most houses when a parent tells the 11-year-old child to sit down, the 11-year-old child sits down. But my house isn't like most houses these days. My house is the no-fly zone for logic, reason and joint parenting.

Adam didn't sit down, so I got up and blocked the door. Adam screamed for Beth. He said that I wouldn't let him leave the room. Then he started hitting me. I went into my 44 year old imitation of Muhammad Ali's rope-a-dope. I had this fantasy that if I let Adam hit me long enough he would work out his anger and frustration, collapse in tears into my arms, and the healing would begin. Let's just say the rope-a-dope worked better for Ali against George Foreman than it did for me. There was no rope and I was the dope.

Beth called the police when I wouldn't unlock the door or let Adam out of the room. She told them I physically assaulted Adam. When the police arrived they separated everyone and talked to each of us individually. Luckily, Adam told the police the truth – I never laid a hand him.

The cop said I was within my rights to keep Adam in the room with me – maybe not the best way to handle the situation but certainly not against the law. The officer even brought Adam over so I could talk to him without Beth hovering overhead. No one was arrested. The official police report stated, "Verbal only. No violence. All okay at this time." Only a police officer used to seeing much worse would characterize my situation as "all okay at this time," but I wasn't about to argue.

Later Adam and I were both on the phone with Jared. Jared was still in Florida. I had called Jared earlier and told him Mom and I was getting divorced. I also told him about my problems with Adam. When Jared asked Adam why he doesn't have dinner with me Adam responded, "Because Mom says she needs me to be with her. She says she doesn't want to be alone." Adam also added that he is sleeping in Mom's bed because "she wants him to."

Adam slept in Beth's bed for the 4th night in a row.

July 19

Jared came home from Florida tonight. Beth had threatened to show up at LaGuardia Airport, but I knew the round trip through

New York area traffic would probably deter her. Tonight was the first time I ever enjoyed the sight of all those cars standing still on the highway. Despite the traffic, I got to the airport on time. Beth wasn't anywhere in sight.

When Jared came off the plane, I was immediately struck by how grown up he looked. He was only gone ten days, but I could have sworn I put a shuffling, headset-wearing, self-absorbed teenager on that plane. The airlines returned a self-assured looking young man who walked with purpose. All that and frequent-flyer miles too.

After Jared and I got home, Adam came outside while I was unloading the car. Adam was cold, but wanted my attention. I guess negative attention is better than no attention.

Adam put me on the witness stand – questioning me like an attorney about things I've said and done. Beth obviously shared a lot of information with him. Adam even questioned me about subjects being discussed by the attorneys. I answered some of his questions; I told him other topics were off limits. After the conversation was over, I decided that *any* further conversation with Adam about the divorce and the reasons for the divorce is off limits.

Later I learned the meaning of Yogi Berra's "It's déjà vu all over again" quote. I was back in the master bedroom listening to Beth tell one of our children what a horrible person I am. The scene was similar to the other night. Only this time, the child was Jared.

Beth ranted, but Jared wasn't having any part of it. For every accusation and name Beth lobbed my way, Jared volleyed back – calmly telling his Mom that nothing leading up to the divorce had anything to do with him. He wasn't taking sides.

For the most part, I stood listening to Beth and Jared with my mouth open but unable to speak. Jared sounded like a parent.

Beth sounded like a child. Jared kept repeating, "None of that matters. Let's just get through this as painlessly as possible." Beth kept repeating, "But Jared, you don't understand…"

But Jared did understand. That was Beth's problem. Jared was too mature. The headset-wearing, self-absorbed teenager had been paying attention the last few years. Beth couldn't get to Jared the way she got to Adam.

Adam, on the other hand, slept in Beth's bed again.

July 20

Jared and I went out, and when we arrived home Adam was sleeping in Beth's bed again. If you're keeping score, tonight makes eight nights in a row. I got in my own bed but couldn't sleep. I decided to write Adam a letter. Here's part of it:

Dear Adam:

It has been one week since you were put in the middle of the problems between your Mom and me.

Since you still don't want to talk normally with me, hang out with me, and go places with me, I thought I would start writing you letters. I may not give them to you for a while – I want you to read them. If I gave them to you now you would probably just throw them away to hurt my feelings. Maybe one day you'll be ready to read them and help me get our relationship back on track.

I know you are angry with me. I know you are scared about Mom and me getting a divorce. But what you have to understand is when people are angry and scared, they should turn to the people they love, the people who love them, for help. You turned to Mom. That's great. But you should also turn to me. I'm your Dad and I can help you if you would just give me a chance.

I would love to work things out with you quickly. Every minute, hour and day that goes by is time we will never get back. We've lost a week, Adam. That's a week we can never get back. The thought of losing any more time with you hurts too much to think about.

Love,
Dad

July 21

The woman I'm involved with, Kelly, had a message waiting for her on the answering machine when she came home from work. The caller called her a whore. He may have said a lot more. But we'll never know because Kelly immediately hit the delete button. Her son was standing next to her. She didn't want him hearing anything else.

July 22

Jared and I left for Washington D.C. this morning. I have a meeting with my boss tomorrow, and I thought a day riding our bicycles around Washington would be a nice distraction. I invited Adam to join us but he said no.

Adam may not have been with us, but I'm pretty sure I was in his thoughts. Kelly got another call from the person who left the "whore" message yesterday. The caller asked, "Did you get my message?" In response to his question Kelly asked one of her own, "Is this an 11-year-old child?" My son said yes, then added, "Stay away from my family you whore bitch."

I can't believe Beth put Adam up to this and gave him Kelly's phone number. She probably even dialed the phone for him.

July 23

Jared called Beth from the hotel in Washington, and Beth asked to talk to me. She said she is out of money. She said she didn't have any money for food. I suggested she cash a check from the insurance company she had in her possession. She said no. I suggested she use her credit card. She said no again.

On the way home from Washington I stopped and bought bread, milk, soda, sandwich meats – even the juice that Beth drinks. Last night Beth said she needed money for food, but the refrigerator was so full I had to rearrange things just to put away the couple of items I bought.

When Jared and I got home about 10:00 p.m. Adam and Beth were in her bed playing Monopoly. Jared said, "If they had food up there they would never leave that room." Too bad Monopoly doesn't include a "Get Out of Mom's Bed Free" card. Not that Adam would use it.

July 25

Dear Adam:

I called you earlier today and you talked to me more then than you had the last few days. I took that as a good sign.

Adam, did I tell you I was sorry? I'm sorry you are in the middle of stuff between Mom and me. I'm sorry we're getting a divorce, and you won't have both your parents living with you anymore. I'm sorry for blocking the door last week. That was wrong.

But most of all I'm sorry Mom has said the things about me she's said. That's wrong too. As I've said, some of the stuff is true. But a lot of it isn't. Kids like to think their parents are perfect. But parents aren't perfect. We just try and do the best we can. I'm sorry you had to hear that I'm not perfect. But even though I'm not perfect I know that I've been a great Dad to you and Jared.

I would give anything for one of your great hugs right now. I miss you so much.

Love,
Dad

July 26

I tried talking to Adam about coming to the mountains for my parent's annual "treat the whole family to a summer vacation" effort. In the past they rented a beach house for one week, but this year they decided the mountains would be a nice change of pace. Our location won't be the only difference. My brother Steve and his wife aren't coming because they just had a baby. My sister Jill, her husband and kids will be in California for his 40th birthday. And I better get used to the idea that Adam won't be there either. He didn't say no when I asked him to come, but his non-verbal communication spoke volumes.

July 29

Beth is using another tool to keep the kids in the middle of our divorce – money. She's taking Jared and Adam's money and telling them I'll pay them back. Tonight she took 30 dollars from Jared and then took both kids to the movies.

Beth is being financially irresponsible – divorce or no divorce. She threw her Macy's bill at me earlier. She said, "Pay this. It is due tomorrow." What could Beth possibly think she's accomplishing by not paying a bill in her name by the due date?

These days Beth is also using her children as communication messengers. She sent Adam into my bedroom earlier asking for $20. She told Jared to tell me she wanted a copy of my paycheck. When I left her Macy's bill on the kitchen table, Beth had Jared deliver it to my room.

Adam is getting colder and nastier. This morning he wouldn't talk to me. When he finally did say something, he accused me of being with Kelly after I told him I was at the office. He even questioned where I'm getting the money for his allowance. I told him if he can't talk nicely, he shouldn't talk to me. He practically laughed in my face.

July 30

Adam slept in Beth's bed again last night – day 16. Jared and I left for the mountains in upstate New York this morning – alone.

July 31

Dear Adam:

Jared and I are at a resort in the mountains with Grandpa and Grandma. You should be here with us. I love you and miss you.

In the last few days you've been very rude to me. You gave me the silent treatment when I tried talking to you. You hung up the phone when I called you. When you did talk to me you were rude and disrespectful. The only time you talked nicely was when you wanted something.

I've had enough Adam. I'm tired of your attitude. I'm not your punching bag. You need to show me some respect.

I know you're mad, upset and scared about the divorce. I also understand, even if you don't, that you are being manipulated. But you have treated me like garbage for two weeks. At first I allowed it so you could get your anger out. I thought it would help us get back on track. But I was wrong. Your behavior is getting worse, not better. I'm done allowing that behavior.

I love you Adam. I can't think about you without crying. But I would rather cry alone than allow you to treat me this way.

Love,
Dad

August 4

Welcome home.

When Jared and I walked through the door this afternoon Beth handed me a note. She wrote that her lawyer said I'm not allowed to lock my bedroom door. The only reason I locked my door was that Beth stole some of my things out of my room after I told her I was moving out September 1st. I had to make sure my clothes were here when I got back from vacation. I almost asked Beth what her lawyer would say if he knew she had been locking her bedroom door for the last three weeks, but I knew she wouldn't appreciate the irony.

Adam refused to talk to me when I came into the house. The atmosphere was so tense; I left after about five minutes. As I walked out the door, Beth yelled that she would call her lawyer if I kept the door locked. Then she called me an asshole in front of the kids. That locked door must really bother her.

When I returned home I tried throwing some dirty laundry into the washing machine. Beth didn't like that either. We started arguing, and she called Adam into the laundry room. Adam called me a fuck face and other names. I finally took my laundry out of the washing machine to avoid a bigger conflict.

Beth must have worked overtime on Adam while I was away. His language and behavior tonight was his worst yet.

P.S. – I don't know where Adam slept when I was away, but tonight he was back in Beth's bed.

August 5

I passed Adam in the hall on my way to bed. "Good night Adam, I love you," the father said. "Fuck you," the son responded.

August 7

Beth's newest form of harassment is to stand over me while I'm eating and yell that I'm not allowed to eat food she bought "for the kids." Pointing out that she bought the food with money from my paycheck only infuriates her more.

Tonight I was dining on a gourmet meal of peanut butter and jelly on rye bread when Beth went into her routine. Since my choice for dinner didn't give her a whole lot to work with, Beth quickly transitioned to my locked bedroom door. As a finale, she brought Adam over to demand I give her more money.

Act two of tonight's performance took place in my bedroom. Jared and Adam were both with me. The kids were on the computer, and I was reading the paper. It was the first time Adam and I spent any "normal" time together in almost one month. Naturally, I locked the door for privacy. The fact that the locked door would also infuriate Beth was just a bonus.

Sure enough, within minutes Beth was banging on the door demanding I open it. She insisted that I am not allowed behind a locked door with the kids. She also decided that my bedroom was "the office," and she had every right to be there. Finally, she left.

Adam slept in her bed again, but that's not the worst of it. Tonight Beth hung up two very sexy, transparent teddies to dry. Adam has been sleeping in her room for weeks. If she wore those things to bed with Adam, she is sicker than I ever imagined.

August 9

I went to Washington D.C. on business and didn't get home until 10:30 p.m. It was still a brutal night.

Beth bothered me about my locked bedroom door. She yelled that I'm not allowed to eat the food in the house. She told the kids that the reason they won't have milk for breakfast is because I'm not giving her money for food. Beth didn't bother mentioning that there is more than $200 in the joint checking account and she spent $60 getting her hair cut and colored earlier today.

When I went upstairs to my room, Jared came with me. On the way up the stairs Adam punched me. I locked him out of the room. Adam pounded on the door for 15 minutes. Jared and I left the house about 11:30 p.m. On the way out Adam punched and cursed me some more.

Once we were out of the house I talked to Jared about a decision I made. I planned on checking into a hotel next week and staying there until my apartment is ready on September 1st. I told Jared I would get a hotel room close by with two double beds so he could sleep over any time he wanted. Thankfully, he understood.

When we returned home my key wouldn't work in my bedroom door. Someone put soap or glue in the lock to keep me out of the room. I finally got the door open and fell asleep about 2:00 a.m.

After Adam finished yelling and cursing at me from outside the door, he went to sleep in Beth's bed again.

August 10

I went to shave with my electric shaver this morning and discovered that someone cut the electrical cord.

That was the last straw. I packed up my clothes and loaded them in the car. I wasn't waiting until next week to move out. Beth heard me banging around and came out to investigate. She saw me packing, smiled, and went back to her room.

Dear Adam:

When I came down to shave this morning I discovered that someone had cut the cord to my electric shaver. I don't know who did it. But I do know it is time to leave the house.

So kiddo, last night was the last night that you and I will spend under the same roof until you are ready to stay with me outside this house. Are you happy about that? On the one hand, you won't have me in your face telling you I love you or talking to you. But on the other hand, you won't have me around to punch and curse. You won't be able to slide ripped pictures underneath my door. How do you feel about that?

I'll be staying in a hotel for the next three weeks until my apartment is ready. I don't know how much I'll be talking to you or seeing you. I can't make you come to the phone. I can't make you answer email. I can't make you go out to dinner with me. I can't make you stay with me.

Adam, I love you and I am always here for you. But I am not here for you to punch or curse. No matter what anyone says, I've been a wonderful father. I deserve your respect. If you are not ready to treat me with respect, I will just love you from a distance.

Love,
Dad

The evening was a very surreal experience. I took both kids shopping so they could buy Beth birthday presents. Her birthday is in six days. Adam picked out a bottle of perfume. Jared's gift choice was pretty interesting – he picked out one of those continuously flowing water over rock contraptions that are supposed to relax and soothe the people around it. I paid for both gifts. Adam acted almost normal the entire evening.

I checked into the hotel after I dropped the kids at the house.

August 11

Jared and I were at the mall last night. He needed some new clothes for school. We were eating pizza when Adam walked up. Adam accused me of stealing money out of his savings account. I told him to talk politely or leave. He refused. Jared and I left instead – but not before Adam kicked me in the leg.

I can't believe Adam thinks I would take his money. Where does he get these ideas? Never mind. That was a stupid question.

August 14

Dear Adam:

    You asked me last night for your allowance and money for cutting the lawn.

    Enclosed is the money for cutting the lawn. I set aside a few dollars for your savings account like I always do. I'm paying you for cutting the lawn because you earned it. If you continue cutting the lawn, I'll continue paying you.

    Your allowance is another story. Allowance is a privilege, not a right. Unfortunately, you've lost this privilege for the disrespectful and rude way you've behaved towards me. I understand you are mad. But that doesn't give you the right to act the way you've acted. You will not get any allowance until you start talking politely and treating me with respect.

    Adam, I will be the happiest Dad around when I can start giving you your allowance again. I love you more than you will ever know. And there is nothing I want more in this world than to be with you. But until you start showing me a little respect, I won't give you any allowance.

Love,
Dad

* * * *

Dr. Davies: He doesn't see you as his father anymore.

Mike: What?

Dr. Davies: Adam doesn't see you as his father anymore. Weren't you going to ask me how he could be so disrespectful? How he could be so rude and abusive

67

given your previously loving father/son relationship?

Mike: So now you're a psychic too?

Dr. Davies: I'm not a psychic. But the change in an alienated child's behavior is the hardest concept for an alienated parent to accept.

The transition from loved and respected Dad to hated and despised Dad happens slowly. Adam was angry with you. He was angry that you ended the marriage, broke up his home and caused him pain. That's normal. It is also normal for a child to act out his anger.

However on top of Adam's normal pre-adolescent anger is another layer of anger. Adam is angry with you for making his mother unhappy and angry. Remember, at this point there are no boundaries separating the alienating parent's emotional perspective from the child's emotional perspective. What she feels, he feels.

In a healthy divorce both parents help the child work through the anger. They let the child express his anger appropriately – within limits. But in alienation the alienating parent doesn't set limits for the child, because she doesn't set limits for herself. The parent's anger reinforces the child's anger and vice versa.

In strict behavioral terms when a behavior is followed by positive reinforcement, or not followed by a negative reinforcement, the likelihood of that behavior continuing increases.

Beth sent Adam all sorts of verbal and non-verbal signals that he could act any way he wanted without consequences. So over the course of the month you watched Adam's behavior get more defiant, oppositional and confrontational. Adam tested the limits and discovered that there were no limits anymore. Beth reinforced Adam's perception by allowing his inappropriate display of anger towards you.

In order for Adam to behave the way he does, he had to stop seeing you as Dad and start seeing you as someone to be despised and disrespected. He had to make the distinction from the father that once was to the father who caused him and his mother all this pain.

Eventually the alienated child doesn't need any more reinforcement from the alienating mother. He acts out on his own. The alienated child may have started out repeating things his mother said, but now he is expressing his own opinions and thoughts. The bond with the alienating mother is extremely strong. She is there for him, and the alienated parent isn't. In the eyes of the child, the alienated father is no longer the father he loved. Now he is the enemy.

Mike: Why is the alienating parent so successful?

Dr. Davies: Because she plays on a child's worst fears. An alienating parent with her own unresolved abandonment issues tells the child that your father is leaving us. On the other hand, she says, "I will never leave you. I'll indulge you and treat you well." The child is vulnerable and wants security. The alienating parent makes the child feel secure. In

69

return, the child helps keep the alienated parent's abandonment fears at bay.

The alienating parent also raises the child's status from that of a child to that of an equal – with all the privileges that go with the elevated status. A child can't ask for anything more, but he learns his security and elevated status are conditional on his unwavering loyalty to the alienating parent and continued rejection of the other parent.

Mike: Are you saying the alienating parent's love is conditional on the child's continued rejection of the other parent?

Dr. Davies: In most cases, yes.

When a parent raises a child with unconditional love, the parent tells the child that no matter what you do, who you are or how you behave, I will still love you.

Unconditional love is a very important concept for a child's healthy emotional development. It gives the child the very powerful message that, "No matter what you do, I will always love, support and be here for you." Unconditional love allows the child to explore his or her world and attempt new things. Whether the child succeeds or fails is irrelevant. Unconditional love gives the child the ability to become self-sufficient, independent and develop the self-confidence to successfully find his or her place in the world.

The last thing an alienating parent wants is for the alienated child to become self-sufficient and independent. A self-sufficient and independent child might have ideas different from her ideas. Different ideas might compromise the alienating parent's ability to control and manipulate the child into remaining loyal to her. She'll do anything to avoid feeling abandoned again – even place conditions on her love for her child.

In conditional love the parent's love for the child is based on the child's ability to please the parent and act in accordance with her wishes. In an alienation situation, the alienating parent is pleased when the child rejects the other parent. She views the rejection as loyalty to her. The parent is happy the child isn't abandoning her and rewards him with love, approval, and privileges commensurate with the child's newly elevated status. The child, worried that his only security may abandon him, continues rejecting the other parent in order to continue receiving the alienating parent's love and approval – thus ensuring his security. The child also enjoys the rewards. He continues rejecting the targeted parent to keep the alienating parent happy and cement his position. The alienated parent and child get caught up in a vicious, unhealthy circle. This circle is very damaging to the child.

Mike: How?

Dr. Davies: The child learns that the only way to ensure his parent's love is to stay angry at, disrespect, and have no contact with, the other parent. In a healthy situation, a parent's love has nothing to do with a child's anger. But an alienating parent needs the child's loyalty to her and anger towards the targeted parent in order to avoid her old abandonment issues. So she makes her love for the child conditional on the child's staying angry and meeting her needs.

A parent who loves conditionally negatively affects a child's sense of self. The child's object relations become skewed. He begins thinking about himself only in terms of how he performs his new role. The child's self-esteem suffers.

Mike: How much of the child's behavior is his anger, and how much of it is the alienating parent's anger?

Dr. Davies: Hard to say. In your case, initially Adam was angry and hurt that his parents were divorcing and that his family, his reality, was breaking apart. That's normal. However, over time children learn to deal with this loss. They build new realities. But Beth didn't let Adam resolve his anger. Instead, she had Adam take on her anger. Her cause became his cause. You also gave Adam another reason to stay angry.

Mike: Are you talking about Kelly?

Dr. Davies: I'm talking about Kelly.

Mike: What role does Kelly play in my situation?

Dr. Davies: No role in terms of parental alienation. The presence of another person, another relationship if you will, in a parental alienation equation is insignificant. All Kelly did was give Beth and Adam justification for their anger and actions. If Kelly didn't exist, Beth and Adam would have found some other justification for their feelings, and you'd be in the same spot you are in today.

Parental alienation does not occur because one spouse establishes a relationship with someone else. Parental alienation occurs because one spouse leaves a marriage and the other spouse has unresolved abandonment and emotional issues. The spouse with the unresolved issues and poor object relations feels incomplete. She makes her child an extension of herself so she can feel whole again.

Mike: Try telling that to an 11 year old.

Dr. Davies: You're right. An 11 year old is too young to understand unresolved abandonment issues and poor object relations. But he does understand betrayal. And remember, an 11 year old thinks concretely. If Mom says, "Dad left us for someone else," the child knows: One, Dad left the house; and two, Dad sees someone else. The child has all the reasons he needs to justify his negative feelings about Dad. A pre-adolescent is too young to understand that divorce is rarely just one person's fault. But that's what the alienating parent presents to the child. The parent reinforces the child's belief that Dad, and Dad alone, broke up his happy home. Naturally, the alienating mother doesn't say anything to the child that might leave the impression that Mom bears some responsibility for the divorce. In fact, the majority of alienating parents would use a third party, or in the absence of a third party any other excuse, to absolve them of any responsibility for the breakdown of the marriage. Essentially, you gave Adam and Beth a big stick to hit you with. You also sent Beth a gift-wrapped excuse for never taking responsibility for her actions.

Mike: So I brought this on myself?

Dr. Davies: No, I didn't say that. Your situation is about a broken trust between a parent and a child. And trust is the foundation of all relationships.

A child's trust in a parent is dependent on the parent's meeting the child's most basic human needs. From the time the child is an infant he trusts Mom and Dad will keep him healthy, safe and secure. The child recognizes that Mom and Dad are a team – working together to keep him fed, warm and dry. If one parent isn't around, the child trusts that the other parent is. If both parents aren't around, the child learns to trust the person or people his parents trust to take care of him until they return.

But in a divorce the team breaks up. Initially, news of the impending divorce shakes the child's world, and his trust in how his world operates, right down to its foundation. When the trust between people is broken or strained, the trust must be restored before the relationship can move forward.

In a healthy divorce, a parent who loses a child's trust because the child feels betrayed or abandoned has the opportunity to regain that trust. Mom and Dad work together to ensure the child feels loved, safe and secure moving forward – despite the change in the family structure. The child's basic beliefs – Mom and Dad are here for me, and I don't have to choose one parent over the other – remain intact. In a parental alienation divorce, the alienating parent doesn't allow the other parent to rebuild the trust. She'll make sure the child continues seeing the parent as untrustworthy – whether he deserves the label or not – and ensure the child's place in her life.

Adam always trusted your honesty, consistency and love. He also trusted that you would provide his security. When you decided to end your marriage, Beth gave Adam information that broke down that trust.

Mike: Adam was upset about the same issue that had Beth initially upset – the divorce. Beth wanted to keep Adam's world status quo, as dysfunctional as that world might have been. I wanted something that Adam couldn't identify with – a life away from his Mom. Adam and Beth wanted the same thing. They were allies. By filing for divorce and moving out, I became the untrustworthy enemy.

Dr. Davies: Yes. You hurt Adam deeply by leaving and subsequently divorcing his mother. His disappointment with you went way beyond anything he had ever experienced. Adam stopped believing you loved him and that you would be there for him. I'm sure Beth reinforced these feelings every chance she got.

Mike: Beth either told Adam about Kelly or let Adam overhear her on the phone with her friends. According to Adam, I lied to "the family" about my relationship with Kelly. Beth reinforced Adam's belief every chance she could. Whenever I told Adam that Mom wasn't telling him the truth about how much money she had or some other subject that Adam had no business being involved in, Beth reminded Adam that I never told him about Kelly. I doubt Beth ever expected me to share information with Adam that was clearly inappropriate for an 11 year old, but her revisionist approach to our family history came in handy every time she wanted Adam to believe that something she said was true and anything I said was a lie.

Dr. Davies: In order to re-establish his relationship with you, Adam needed to learn to trust you all over again. But unlike a parent in a healthy divorce, you didn't have the chance to restore Adam's trust and rebuild the relationship. Now he won't give you the opportunity to hurt him again.

Mike: What roles do a child's maternal and paternal bonds play in the concept of trust?

Dr. Davies: Big roles.

A child's healthy maternal bond is initially based on dependence, care giving and trust. Before the child ever leaves the womb he or she is dependent on the mother for nourishment and good health. After the child is born, he or she sees the mother as the parent most responsible, and often most available, for bathing, changing, and feeding. Children with healthy maternal bonds learn to trust in the first few months of life that Mom will meet their needs.

A child's healthy maternal bond naturally changes as early as ages two, three and four. The bond can change even earlier if other caretakers – a grandparent, babysitter or day-care worker – enter the picture. At these ages children start flexing their independence – feeding themselves, using the bathroom alone and venturing out into the world for short periods of time without Mom or Dad in tow. In traditional two parent homes, two-, three- and four-year-old girls begin looking at Mom as their role model. Boys at these ages begin looking at Dad as their role model. At the same time both sexes begin shifting some of their trust from Mom to Dad.

For boys their healthy maternal bond naturally changes over time, while the corresponding healthy paternal bond grows stronger. When older boys start experiencing physical and emotional changes, their desire to identify more with Dad and less with Mom accelerates. Eventually, the paternal bond is as strong as the maternal bond. Both bonds are healthy.

Mike: Adam was only 11 when I moved out of the house. I guess his paternal bond with me wasn't strong enough at that age to withstand Beth's pressure to choose a side. Adam put it best one day after I suggested that Mom wasn't being totally honest with him. "Mom wouldn't lie to me," he said. "She gave birth to me." How do you explain to an 11-year-old boy that there is no connection between giving birth and telling the truth?

Dr. Davies: The answer is simple. You can't. For Beth, having Adam's trust in so many different ways was like putting money in the bank. When she needed to make a withdrawal in order to keep from feeling totally abandoned, she knew she had enough trust saved up in the account to ensure that Adam would keep away all her old abandonment fears.

A Family's Heartbreak

6

Pressure to Conform

August 17

JARED SHOWED ME A SCHEDULE he developed that would have him spending seven out of 14 days with each parent. Jared's schedule works something like the World Series – two games on Team A's home field, the next three games on Team B's home field, and then back to Team A's field for the final two games. According to Jared's schedule each "week" begins on Monday. This puts him with each parent on alternating weekends.

I think Jared's schedule is great. Let's see how Beth responds.

August 21

For Father's Day Beth and the kids gave me four tickets to today's Yankee game. Adam would not come to the game without Beth. I refused to take Beth. Jared and I went to the game alone.

I've been going to Yankee Stadium since the 1960s. Dad always took me to the stadium when I was a kid. One time when I was about Adam's age, Dad and I went to the stadium in February or March to buy tickets for a game later that year. Somehow Dad talked his way past a security guard so we could see where our seats were. We walked out from a tunnel to the field level box seats behind home plate. The stadium's enormity and stillness overwhelmed me. The New York Giants played their football games at the stadium back then, and that day the yard lines were still visible on the field. Dad and I stood there, the only two people in a stadium that held more the 60,000 fans. We looked out at the monuments in center field. We looked at the dugouts. We looked up at the famous Yankee Stadium façade that lined the roof. We never found our seats, but it didn't matter. My Dad was a Yankee fan. I was a Yankee fan. We were alone in the House that Ruth Built. Call it a Kodak moment without the camera.

I wanted to share the Yankees with my sons the way Dad shared them with me. I wanted Jared and Adam to have their own Yankee memories. Tonight Jared watched me sell his Mom's and Adam's tickets to a scalper. He watched me wipe away tears throughout most of the game because Adam wasn't with us. Jared's single, most powerful memory of tonight's game will probably be the sound of his own voice repeating over and over, "It will be all right, Dad." Not exactly the memory I had in mind.

August 25

Beth made plans for Jared to stay at a friend's house tonight even though Jared was supposed to be with me. Beth never discussed the sleepover with me. She never even discussed it with Jared. She just told Jared about it a few minutes before they had to leave. Jared called me and asked what he should do.

Since Jared and I didn't have plans, I told him to go and have fun – and don't feel guilty.

August 28

My company had its annual summer picnic at a water theme park today. I had tickets for Jared and Adam but Adam refused to come with us. Jared brought along his friend from the sleepover instead.

After dropping Jared's friend off at the end of the day, Jared shared something with me that had obviously been on his mind. He said that Beth "decided" the following about his schedule:

- Jared will only stay with me on Wednesday, Friday and Saturday nights because that works best for her.

- Jared will spend Thanksgiving with her.

I told Jared not to worry about the schedule. Beth can't win this one. Then Jared reported that Adam is still sleeping in Beth's bed. I guess she's winning that one.

August 29

Beth is putting pressure on Jared about his schedule – even though we're already adhering to it.

Jared reported that Beth said if he leaves with me on days that she considers to be "her days," she will punish him when he gets back – no friends over to the house, no computer time, no video games, and so on.

According to Jared, Beth also said she won't let him in the house if he shows up on "Dad's days." He is no longer allowed to take the bus back to the house and wait for me to pick him up after work.

Jared wasn't too concerned about any of this. Thankfully, he has plenty of experience dealing with Beth's punishment threats and her track record of never following through.

August 30

Dear Adam:

I love you and I miss you. But you already know that.

I hope you had a good day at the first day of school today. I would love to hear all about it. I would love to talk to you about a lot of things. And we will. I promise.

I'm thinking about you Adam. I'm always thinking about you. We'll get through this soon. I know it. Then we can start doing the stuff we used to do together.

All my love always,
Dad

September 4

As I drove over to pick Jared up, he called me in the car. He wanted to take his old Nintendo system over to the apartment. This was the original Nintendo system. It hadn't even been out of its box in years because Jared and Adam had the newer Nintendo systems hooked up to the television. But Beth didn't want Jared taking the system.

Jared decided to take his game anyway. When Beth saw Jared walking out of the house with it, she became physically aggressive– grabbing at Jared's arms and pushing him in an effort to get him to drop the box. I had to tell Beth to take her hands off Jared, or I would call the police. She finally let him go, and we left.

Before all the excitement over the Nintendo system, I had asked Jared to bring over his lunch container so I could make his lunch and send it to school with him. I really didn't think Beth would object. Guess what? Beth objected. Jared will "brown bag" it tomorrow.

Whoever pinned the nickname "Material Girl" on Madonna never met Beth.

September 6

Jared reported that he wised off to Beth today. Under normal circumstances, my son wouldn't volunteer such self-incriminating information, but circumstances in my dysfunctional family are anything but normal.

What made this episode noteworthy was Beth's response. According to Jared Beth said, "Don't disrespect me. Your father disrespected me for years." Beth then proceeded, according to Jared, to call me a liar, abuser, cheater, garbage, and bastard – her usual litany – in front of Jared, Adam and their two friends.

September 9

I called Adam tonight. I missed him. He came to the phone, but Beth sat with her ear to the extension listening to every word. Beth can't even eavesdrop without having something to say. After about two minutes, she started yelling at me. I yelled back that she should get off the phone. When she didn't, I hung up.

Adam called back later. He tried justifying why he doesn't want to talk to me or see me. But I might as well have been listening to Beth. She's really programmed Adam's every response. I tried talking logically and rationally, explaining why he shouldn't be in the middle between Beth and me. Why he deserves to have great relationship with both his parents. But he is only 11. Adam got frustrated when I told him anything that contradicted what Beth told him. By the end of the conversation he was crying. He called me a bastard and hung up.

September 10

Jared was over tonight. When he called Beth for something, I asked him to ask for Adam and then hand me the phone. I don't like putting Jared in the middle, but it's getting harder and harder to go through Beth to get to Adam only to give her the pleasure of turning me away on his behalf.

When Adam heard my voice he asked, "What are you doing on the phone?" I told him I missed him and wanted to talk to him. He hung up on me.

September 13

I stopped by the gym before picking up Jared. I bought Adam one of the breakfast muffins we used to enjoy when we went to the gym together. I also had a letter I'd written to Adam.

When Jared came out to the car, I asked him to go back in the house and give Adam the muffin and letter. He did, and then Adam came running out of the house with the letter in his hand. He ripped up the letter in front of me. When he saw tears in my eyes, he said, "Are you going to cry now, you big baby?" Jared and I drove away.

Adam left the muffin in the house. My son may be alienated, but he's not stupid. Those muffins are delicious – far too tasty to waste on a public performance.

September 14

Dear Adam:

    I tried talking to you on the phone today, but you hung up on me. Come on Adam. How long is this going to go on? Today is two months to the day since that horrible night when you got dragged between Mom and me. Remember that night? It was the worst night of my life. Since I'm 44, we're talking about the worst night in almost 16,000 nights.

    Adam, part of growing up and loving other people is forgiveness – the ability to forgive. Whether you are right or wrong to feel the way you do doesn't matter. People who are part of a family forgive each other because they love each other.

    I'll tell you again. You don't belong between Mom and me. It is not your responsibility to stick up for her and be mad at me when she says I did something (or didn't do something) that she doesn't like. Mom is an adult and can take care of herself. She has a lawyer to take care of her too.

    You deserve to feel good about talking to me and spending time with me without feeling like you are betraying Mom.

    Think about this kiddo. Then think about forgiveness. You are a very smart kid. You're very sensitive too. I know you'll figure it out one day. I just want you to figure it out sooner rather than later. We've lost too much time already.

I love you and miss you more than you will ever know.

Dad

* * * *

Mike:
How is Jared able to avoid Beth's alienation campaign and pressure to support her position when Adam can't?

Dr. Davies:
It would appear Jared is to your family what Switzerland was to World War II. Jared declared his neutrality and never wavered.

Mike:
But how?

Dr. Davies:
Jared is a teenager. At his age a child has a better sense of self than an 11–year-old child. Jared also has a good grip on reality, good boundaries and the ability to stay objective and emotionally distant from the chaos swirling around him.

Don't get me wrong – his situation is far from perfect. Jared suffers every time he is with his Mom and brother. He probably feels like the odd man out. But overriding whatever uncomfortable feelings Jared has is a healthy respect for, and obedience to, both parents. He figured out that choosing one parent over the other was a no-win situation for him. So Jared made the conscious choice not to make a choice.

Mike:
But Beth didn't want Jared to stay neutral. By maintaining his neutrality Jared really did make a choice. He chose not to side with Beth.

Dr. Davies:
Despite Beth's campaign to discredit you, Jared stays an equal distance between both his parents. He knows if he moves too far toward Mom he will hurt Dad. If he moves too far toward Dad he will hurt Mom. By staying in the middle he doesn't hurt either one of you – or himself. Jared did the only thing a child in his position could do. He

86

established a position an equal distance between both his parents and stood his ground.

Mike: How does a child resist the kind of pressure that Beth put on Jared?

Dr. Davies: A child's ability to resist an alienating parent's pressure to conform is directly related to his stage of emotional development. As a child matures, he individuates, or begins seeing himself as separate from his family. The child will start defining himself based on factors such as peer relationships, ability, intellect and how he feels others accept and like him. This is a normal and healthy process. At an earlier stage of the process a child's individuation might take the form of going out alone with friends or sleeping at someone else's house. Later in the process the child steps away from defining himself emotionally and psychologically in terms of his family. At this point the child is better able to resist an alienating parent's pressure to think what she thinks and feel what she feels.

Mike: What happens to the relationship between the alienating parent and the child who refuses to be alienated?

Dr. Davies: Their relationship changes. The alienating parent stops trusting the child because in her mind, the child consorts with the enemy. She still feels responsible for the child, but she doesn't bestow upon this child the same status she bestows on the alienated child. In a sense, one child travels first class while the other child travels coach. Mom makes sure both kids get where they need to go, but

Mom gives one child perks and upgrades while the other child gets a bag of peanuts.

In spite of this treatment, the alienating parent and non-alienated child are still mother and son. That bond doesn't break easily. But their future together will depend on their ability to form a relationship without the alienated parent as the central character in both their lives. They won't have a close, loving relationship unless they do.

Mike: So what happens to the relationship between siblings like Jared and Adam when they have such vastly different views of the two people who were the most important people in their lives?

Dr. Davies: Siblings face the same challenge. They must find common ground that they can enjoy without Mom or Dad as part of the equation.

Mike: Do most kids discover this common ground?

Dr. Davies: That depends. At least one child must be smart enough and mature enough to step back and look at the family dynamics intellectually. If both children look at the situation emotionally, all they'll see is their own loss and pain. They won't be able to see through their emotions in order to find the common ground. One of them must be emotionally and psychologically independent of the family so he can show the other child the way.

Mike: How common is it for a parent to alienate one child but not the other?

Dr. Davies: That really depends on each child's age and development. In my experience most alienated children are younger than twelve years old. Children from age three to twelve are most susceptible to alienation because they haven't completely developed their sense of self and emotionally separated from their family. An alienating parent and primary caregiver can influence these children very easily. Older children have developed better coping skills. They're able to separate themselves from the family. Parents aren't nearly as successful at alienating older children as they are at alienating younger children.

Mike: Jared is my only source of information about Adam. How do I, or any alienated parents, satisfy the need to hear something, anything, about the alienated child without putting too much pressure on the non-alienated child?

Dr. Davies: Who says the alienated parent's needs should come before the child's needs? In a perfect world the child doesn't get any pressure to report on a brother or sister. But in a perfect world there isn't parental alienation either. So the alienated parent must balance his or her needs against what's best for the child. If you must ask questions, keep the questions as casual, non-confrontational and benign as possible. In addition:

- Don't make the child choose sides.

- Do be upbeat and happy so the child doesn't take on additional worries or concerns.

- Don't put the child in the middle.

- Do keep repeating that everything will be okay.

- Don't use the child as a messenger.

- Do allow the child to bring up his Mom, Dad or sibling in the normal course of conversation without worrying about how you'll react to the reference.

- Don't ask the child for advice on what to do about Mom, Dad or his sibling.

- Do encourage the development of the child's normal, healthy relationship with Mom or Dad.

- Don't make disparaging comments about Mom or Dad.

7

Living with Alienation

September 15

I GAVE A COURT-ORDERED ATTORNEY, Phillip Crawford, a retainer today to represent Jared and Adam. The kids need an attorney since Beth and I don't agree on anything as it relates to them – especially counseling for Adam. Crawford will speak for Jared and Adam in court and represent their positions.

During our meeting I asked the guy if he had ever heard of parental alienation. He said yes, but he didn't sound too convincing. Time will tell. The next step is for Crawford to meet his new clients.

September 16

I called Adam and wished him a Happy (Jewish) New Year. He responded, "Go away." Then he hung up the phone.

September 18

Beth had one of her patented meltdowns today.

When I dropped Jared off at the house this morning, Beth was waiting. She knew I was going away for the weekend with Kelly, and she wasn't about to let me go without a proper send-off. She screamed that she was going to sue me for alienation of affection. Then she screamed at Jared – threatening to give him proof that I'm a horrible father and person. Jared looked at Beth like she was from another planet.

I backed out of the driveway, but Beth held the car door open and refused to let go. She kept harassing me and yelling at Jared. At the top of the driveway, she hopped into the car and wouldn't get out until I called the police.

I called Jared a couple of hours later to see how he was doing. Jared reported that Beth never said another word once they were inside the house.

September 20

Beth and I were in court today. The judge issued temporary alimony and child support orders.

After court I picked up Jared at the house. Adam came out and demanded money for a Boy Scout outing. Adam doesn't ask for anything anymore. Phrases like "May I please have…" or even "Will you please give me…" are no longer in his vocabulary. These days he uses phrases like, "You owe me…" and "Give me (fill in the blank) now." Despite Adam's rude approach, I wrote a check for his outing. Unfortunately I committed a cardinal sin before handing over the check – I asked Adam where he was going with the Boy Scouts.

In response, he called me a "dumb ass." I told him to apologize or he wasn't getting the check. Beth, who had followed Adam out to the car, contributed her two cents. "He's probably going to spend the money on his girlfriend instead," she offered. Adam followed up Beth's helpful comment by calling me a "fat fuck." I had heard enough. I ripped up the check and tried leaving but Adam wouldn't let Jared close the car door. For the second time in three days I had to threaten to call the police just to get out of the driveway. As I drove away Adam ran alongside the car giving me the finger.

September 21

After talking to Beth tonight, Jared delivered the following two messages:

- Beth wants $30 to take the kids for haircuts.

- Adam doesn't like the school clothes I bought him, and Beth says I must return them.

Wasn't I just in court yesterday watching the judge issue temporary alimony and child support orders? The agreement we both signed in court also says Beth is responsible for returning the clothes if Adam doesn't like them. The court's orders are less than two days old and Beth is already making believe they don't exist.

September 26

Last night I tried calling the kids from 9:40 p.m. until 10:45 p.m. Beth must have taken the phone off the hook – the line was busy. When I finally got through, I talked to Jared for a couple of minutes. Then I asked him to put Adam on the phone. Here is our exchange:

Mike:	Hi Adam.
Adam:	What do you want?
Mike:	First I want to tell you I love you.
Adam:	Shut up.
Mike:	Cousins Scott and Susan invited us over this weekend for dinner. Would you like to go?

Adam hung up the phone without responding.

September 27

I found out today that Beth is taking Adam to see a domestic violence counselor. I was livid when I found out. Whom should I call first – the counselor, my attorney – Lisa Slater, or Phil Crawford – the kids' attorney? The court's temporary custody orders clearly state that Beth and I should be making joint decisions about the kids' health care, religion and education. Further, we're supposed to notify each other about doctor appointments, school conferences, etc. Beth didn't consult with me before taking Adam to a domestic violence counselor, and she certainly didn't give me the date and time of the appointment. Lisa drew the short straw.

When I got off the phone with Lisa, it was the counselor's turn. We talked for about 50 minutes. I told him Adam is not a victim of domestic violence. I also told him Beth pulled Adam into the divorce and deliberately destroyed our relationship. The guy seemed nice enough. He apologized for not calling me sooner (he has seen Adam twice) and promised to keep me informed of Adam's progress. Most important, he said he would try and repair my damaged relationship with Adam. If this guy can get through to

Adam, I don't care if he is a domestic violence counselor. Nor will I care what he believes about me.

September 28

Jared and I planned on getting haircuts tonight. But Jared called me at work and said Beth was taking Adam for a haircut this evening. Since we all use the same hairdresser, all the players would be in place for a potential scene.

It took me about five seconds to decide Jared and I didn't need haircuts *that badly*. Later, I heard Jared on the phone repeating, "I don't know." He must have said it five or six times. After Jared hung up he said Beth kept asking him when I was taking him for a haircut. I guess she was disappointed we didn't show up tonight.

October 1

Jared asked Beth if she would let him come over at 11:00 p.m. tonight and sleep over. Technically, tonight is Beth's night. But we're spending Sunday with family in Connecticut. Jared wants an early start so he can spend more time with his cousins.

I've known Beth longer than Jared, so I knew this answer before he ever asked the question. When Jared got off the phone I told him I would pick him up at the house Sunday morning.

October 6

On the way to school this morning Jared asked me for money for tomorrow's school activity – even though he'll be at the house with Beth tonight. I gave Jared the money, but wondered aloud why he didn't just ask his Mom for the money later. He responded, "She'll just tell me to ask you."

I also touched base with Adam's domestic violence counselor today. He saw Adam for the third time last Friday. In a nutshell he reported Adam:

- Is very angry and very stubborn. I should prepare myself for a long process.

- Sees himself as an avenger – he is punishing me because he believes I abused Beth.

- Believes I abused him – even though he couldn't give the counselors any specific examples of abuse.

- Is mad at Phil Crawford because the attorney suggested Adam should have a relationship with me.

- Is "probably" mad at the counselor because the counselor suggested he should have a relationship with me.

- May not come back again because "he doesn't want to." The counselor tried prevailing upon Beth to bring Adam back, but Beth said, "If he doesn't want to come back, I can't make him."

October 7

I called Jared after school. Adam answered the phone. I asked for Jared and Adam hung up. I called again, asked for Jared, and Adam hung up. We repeated this stupid routine at least 20 times. I felt like Bill Murray in *Groundhog Day*. Finally Jared picked up the phone. He had just walked in the door. Adam wouldn't even tell me Jared wasn't home.

October 8

I called the principal of Adam's elementary school this morning. I'm not receiving any information that normally goes home to parents.

The principal understood my situation and said he would put aside everything that goes home with Adam. He even gave me my own little folder in the school office. He also arranged a parent/teacher conference for me.

After I left the principal's office, I was angry with Beth for not giving me copies of Adam's report cards and progress reports. Then I got mad at Adam for not telling me about Back-to-School night. Then my anger with both of them turned to humiliation. I realized I had just asked a total stranger for information about my own son. The guy is responsible for hundreds of kids, yet he knows more about Adam's day-to-day life then I do.

October 11

Jared is sick. Beth kept him home from school. She's supposed to call me and tell me when Jared stays home sick, but she doesn't.

She also took him to a walk-in clinic tonight, and the doctor prescribed an antibiotic. But rather than go get the prescription filled and give Jared the medicine right away, Beth is making Jared wait until tomorrow night for me to fill the prescription. According to Jared, Beth said filling the prescription was "my responsibility."

I tried calling Beth. I was going to tell her to get the prescription filled first thing in the morning, and I would pay for it. Beth picked up the phone, heard my voice, and hung up before I could say anything.

October 12

Jared is still home sick. Naturally, Beth never told me. I heard it from Jared when I called him for our normal after school conversation. Jared promised to call me when he is sick in the future. Once again, the child is acting like the adult while the adult acts like the child.

October 13

Jared was very upset when he got in the car tonight. He tried bringing back some clothes to the apartment that had inadvertently ended up at the house. He ended up in a tug-of-war with Beth over a pair of pants.

Beth the Material Girl did not want Jared leaving the house with the clothes. Maybe she doesn't want to use her child support to buy Jared clothes. Or maybe she doesn't like doing laundry. I don't know. But I do know that Jared was so upset over the incident that he didn't want to go back in the house and give Adam something I had for him.

October 14

I haven't been very happy with Jared and Adam's legal representation.

Despite Phil Crawford's promise one month ago to "get right on this case," I feel that he's dragging his feet. He let Beth put him off for three weeks before finally bringing Adam in to meet him. It also seems that my attorney responds to his letters and calls the same day. But when we contact him, we're lucky if Crawford responds the same week. He's supposed to facilitate the appointment of a psychologist for court-ordered evaluations. The evaluations are necessary so the future court-ordered therapist knows what he or she is dealing with. We can't get to the therapy without the evaluations. We can't get to the evaluations without an evaluator. And we can't get to an evaluator with the attorney for the minor children taking three weeks to meet with his clients and days to return a phone call.

This guy has a sweet deal. His clients are children. They don't know their lawyer is slowing up the process. And unless they're rock stars, kids typically don't call up adults in positions of authority and accuse them of not doing their jobs.

October 16

Beth had a major meltdown this morning. On a one-to-ten scale of hysterical behavior, today's episode rates a 20.

Today is a travel day for Jared. When he wakes up on travel days and he isn't in school he calls the parent with whom he is not residing. For me, the call is a request to come pick him up. For Beth, the call alerts her that I'll be dropping him off soon. Beth rarely picks Jared up. According to Beth, Jared's 15-minute commute between households is also my responsibility.

This morning Beth called at 11:00 a.m. and again at 12:00 p.m. looking for Jared. Both times he was sleeping, and I said so. The second time she demanded that I wake him up and bring him back to her house. I refused – reminding her that Jared was sick all week and could use the sleep.

Beth called twice more. She threatened to file motions. She threatened to send the police over to "escort her son home." I hung up on her both times.

Jared woke up at 12:20 p.m. He called Beth. After showering and eating breakfast, he was back at her house by 1:15 p.m. As usual, I drove him over.

One time when the phone rang, I picked it up expecting to hear Beth screaming, but I heard Adam's voice instead. He wanted money out of his savings account. Unfortunately for Adam, I'm the guardian on his custodial account so he needs my permission.

I told Adam that until he starts treating me with respect the money in his savings account will sit there collecting interest.

We went back and forth. Adam accused me of spending his money on Kelly. From the "oh-how-far-we've-fallen-department," Adam argued that he does treat me with respect since he no longer comes out to curse at me when I pick up Jared. For good measure, Adam also threw in that I was keeping Jared from Beth on "her day."

I stayed on the phone until Adam cursed at me. Then I told my respectful 11-year-old son I loved him and hung up.

* * * *

Dr. Davies: How long has it been now?

Mike: Three months.

Dr. Davies: In many ways your situation is similar to a loss due to death or an unwanted divorce. You feel pain over your lost emotional attachment with Adam. Anyone who has lost the physical presence of someone they cared about suffers in a similar way.

Mike: So?

Dr. Davies: So you have to go through the same stages of denial/disbelief, anger, bargaining and grief that all emotionally healthy people go through when dealing with loss in order to get to the final stage –

acceptance. These stages are progressive. You must finish one stage before moving on to the next.

Mike: I'm nowhere near acceptance.

Dr. Davies: I know. At this point you're in the denial/disbelief stage. You still can't believe that your once loving, sensitive, affectionate child is so rude, disrespectful, cold and even sadistic towards you today.

The denial/disbelief stage is a coping mechanism. Quite simply, in this stage a person denies the loss of a loved one. Denial is not accepting reality – a reality that is too painful to deal with all at once. This stage allows a person to function. A person who suffers the death of a loved one still must make funeral arrangements and take care of other family members. If the person didn't deny the new reality that the loved one is gone forever – the loss would be too intolerable to accept. He or she wouldn't be able to function and complete even the simplest tasks.

In your situation no one died. However, the notion that your loving, caring child has turned against you is too intolerable to accept. You deny this new reality and still practice old behaviors such as asking the child to go out for ice cream, a movie or a bike ride. Denying Adam's position allows you to fulfill your other personal and professional responsibilities.

You'll deny this new reality for a while, but eventually you'll recognize it and stop inviting Adam places because the negative consequences of offering the invitation – the cursing and getting hung up on – are so consistent. It's hard to accept that your child is gone from your life.

An emotionally healthy person doesn't stay in denial very long. He moves into anger. "Why did this happen," he asks repeatedly? A person in the anger stage can stay angry for years. The person can also move past the anger stage, but come back to it – over and over again. The anger stage commonly associated with loss allows a person to express himself at something that was taken away from him. He may direct, or misdirect, his anger at people, places or objects. An alienated parent will direct his anger at the alienating parent and blame her for his loss.

You can't predict how long the anger will last. But the more quickly the person gets through the anger the better.

The bargaining stage is the next stage of loss. In the bargaining stage the person tries rationalizing everything that has happened to him. He starts bargaining with himself. "If only I had stayed in the marriage, this wouldn't have happened," the alienated Dad says to himself. "If only I had left five minutes sooner, I would have arrived in time to call a doctor and save his life," the grieving wife thinks. A person who has suffered a loss, any kind of loss, needs to move through the anger and bargaining stages in order to grieve, mourn the loss of what was and move to the final tage – acceptance.

Acceptance is particularly hard for an nated parent. A loving, caring, sensitive child is an angry, bitter extension of the alienating . The love the alienated parent and child shared is gone. The alienated parent must integrate the reality of the lost child into his day-to-day life and resume his daily activities with the knowledge that his child won't be part of those activities anymore. As hard as accepting this new reality is, acceptance is ultimately in the alienated parent's best interest.

Mike: How does any alienated parent work through the anger? The child isn't dead. There isn't the finality or closure in parental alienation that you find in death.

Dr. Davies: An alienated parent may direct his anger at the alienating parent, but he can't take out his anger on the alienating parent. He needs to find an appropriate release for the anger. Exercise and physical activity are appropriate releases. Beating up the alienating parent isn't an appropriate release. Talking about the situation to parents, brothers, sisters and close friends is appropriate. Yelling at the child isn't appropriate. Each person has to find his or her own appropriate release – volunteer work, art, construction – the release mechanism depends on the person.

Mike: How does an alienated parent ever reach acceptance when the child keeps jerking the parent back into anger? Adam needs to know my love for him is consistent and unconditional – even though he acts the way he does. But every time I show him, I'm punched, cursed or hung up on. Then I get angry all over again.

Dr. Davies: Exactly. The consequences of showing that consistency – the, punching, cursing and getting hung up on – are too negative. You need other ways to remind Adam you love him without putting yourself in that position. For example, you can send him emails or letters. Adam may delete the email or rip up the letter without reading it, but you won't witness it. You have to remind Adam you still care without putting yourself in a position that leads back into the anger.

Emotionally healthy people also avoid the anger by staying emotionally detached from the situation. Think about your relationship with your son intellectually. Remember how you got here. You continue telling the child, "I love you. I care about you." But for every few minutes or hours per week you deliver these positive messages, the alienating parent spends the rest of the week delivering negative messages such as, "He abused and abandoned us." The alienating parent draws on nuclear reaction-level energy to make sure the child stays alienated from the other parent. She never gets tired, lets her guard down or takes a break. The parent constantly looks for new and creative ways to reinforce the child's position against the targeted parent. The odds are really stacked in the alienating parent's favor. You can't have high hopes that your message will penetrate the child's constantly refortified defenses and lead to something positive.

Mike: Are you suggesting I stop wasting my time?

Dr. Davies: Absolutely not. When Adam physically and emotionally distances himself from Beth he will look back on factual information – your phone calls, emails and invitations – in an entirely different light.

Adam is not three or four years old. When an adult who was alienated at three or four looks back, he or she doesn't have the memories or bond with the alienated parent that a child alienated at 11 or 12 years old has. The younger child may have some vague recollection about this person who once lived in the house, but unless the alienated parent somehow remained a constant presence in the child's life after the breakup of the family, the child's memories of those early years are gone. Adam will remember your efforts. He may not acknowledge them until he is physically and emotionally able to acknowledge them, but he will remember them.

Mike: For me the most frustrating part of all this is the "damned if you do, damned if you don't" element of parental alienation. If I put myself out there, I'm beat up emotionally and have nothing to show for it – not even my own emotional health. If I don't put myself out there, Beth tells Adam, "Your father never calls. I told you he abandoned you."

Dr. Davies: Your "damned if you do, damned if you don't" description is the essence of severe parental alienation. In severe cases the alienated parent's actions are irrelevant. The alienating parent is a master at manipulating any situation in order to make the alienated parent look bad. There is literally nothing the alienated parent can do.

This is where a skilled mental health professional can enter the picture and do some good. A good psychologist will challenge the child's reality and point out that there is no substance to the alienated child's perception of the truth – even though the alienating parent and child believe it. If a professional can separate the child from the alienating parent, the professional can make the child face reality. But the alienated parent doesn't have that opportunity. The child hangs up on the parent before the parent can say one word.

Mike:

Does Adam ever feel guilty over the way he treats me?

Dr. Davies:

The relationship you had with Adam is buried somewhere underneath his anger. The alienated child may occasionally feel guilty about his behavior, but at this point he is very adept at letting his anger wash over his guilt. Unfortunately, anger is a wonderful defense mechanism. Anger can cover up anything and keep two people apart. A person doesn't have warm, loving feelings about someone he or she is angry at.

Mike:

So Adam is stuck in the anger stage rather than accept the reality that has Mom and Dad divorced?

Dr. Davies:

Adam uses anger as a coping mechanism. Remember, the alienating parent with the damaged object relations and fear of abandonment is using the child to keep her whole. Beth won't allow Adam to move through the anger stage and reach acceptance, because if Adam accepted the breakdown of his family and a new reality, that reality would include you. Then Beth's unresolved abandonment issues would kick in again. Beth uses Adam's anger to keep away her unresolved issues. Adam uses his anger to cope with his guilt. Adam's anger is the single stone that kills two birds.

8

Looking for Help

October 18

BETH CALLED ME AT WORK. She was very upset. Jared didn't get off the school bus, and she didn't know where he was.

Jared stayed after school for a meeting. He tried calling Beth but either she didn't hear the phone ring, or she didn't turn on the answering machine before going out. Or maybe she thought I was calling and deliberately didn't pick up.

My conversation with Beth was the first civil conversation we've had in three months. I thought maybe the conversation could be an icebreaker. I called her back to ask if we could start working together for the sake of the kids, but I never got the chance. After talking about Jared for a second, I asked Beth if we could build on our earlier civil conversation. Beth responded that she was on another call and she had to get back to her "other caller." Then she hung up.

Later I had Jared call Adam to the phone. I told Adam I was dropping something off at the house for Jared. "Would you like to go out for ice cream," I asked? He hung up the phone without responding.

October 19

I had my weekly conversation with Adam's domestic violence counselor today. He's not seeing Adam until next week, so he didn't have anything new to report. He did, however, ask me about the incident between Beth and Jared last week – when Beth tried to stop Jared from bringing some clothes back to the apartment.

Beth told Mr. Domestic Violence that Jared pushed and punched her. No way, I said. Jared would never get physically aggressive with Beth. I remembered Beth pushing Jared and grabbing at his arms last month when she didn't want him leaving the house with his old Nintendo system. If anything, I told him, Beth got physically aggressive with Jared over the pants. She just turned around their roles when telling the story to portray herself as the victim.

Jared is the most non-aggressive kid I know. When I coached his basketball team, I couldn't even get him to fight for a rebound.

October 22

Today the guidance counselor at Adam's school told me about a program she runs for kids dealing with divorce. I explained that I had to notify Adam's attorney and Beth's attorney (and get Beth's permission) before Adam could participate in her program. I liked the idea of Adam talking with other kids going through similar situations. I told the counselor I'd call her once everyone was on board.

October 25

I had my first meeting today with Dr. Andrew Stone, the court-appointed psychologist doing psychiatric evaluations on everyone in the family. These evaluations are necessary before the judge will order therapy for Adam. I gave the good Dr. Stone a copy of my journal for background.

October 26

Adam is nothing if not consistent. He hung up the phone today when I tried talking to him.

I'm nothing if not consistent too. After calling Adam I made my weekly call to the domestic violence counselor.

The counselor didn't have a whole lot to report. Adam only agreed to come to his most recent appointment if it was *Beth's appointment,* and he attended as a spectator. The counselor also thinks Adam held Beth up for five dollars to attend.

The three of them talked mostly about family issues and school. Adam's relationship with me came up in their discussion, but wasn't the focus of their discussion.

October 29

Jared was missing in action again today. His MIA status prompted Beth to talk civilly to me for the second time in ten days. Beth better be careful. Too many of these conversations and she may be forced to acknowledge I'm not the toxic person she's convinced herself, and Adam, I must be.

Once Beth located Jared she called me to tell me he was on his way home. This time I did not try "building" on our earlier conversation. I thanked her for calling and said goodbye.

October 30

Adam was in the garage when I picked up Jared. I gave Jared a letter to give him. Jared handed Adam the letter, and we both watched Adam rip the letter in half. There was only one flaw in Adam's performance – the letter wasn't from me. When I told Adam the letter was from his grandparents he let out an embarrassed chuckle and continued ripping up the letter as if he knew it was from his grandparents all along.

I honestly believe Adam thinks this whole situation is some sort of giant game – a test of wills. Unfortunately for Adam, he doesn't realize that his idea of winning is actually losing and vice versa. And he won't listen to anyone who knows better.

November 4

Jared and I went shopping for sneakers today. We didn't see anything we liked but Jared hit me up for a book and a model. I understand why Jared wanted the book – he goes through books like someone with a hand-held video game goes through batteries. However I didn't understand why Jared wanted the model. He never builds models. But he said he wanted to build the model with me. He called it "good father and son bonding time."

Jared will never know how much a comment like that meant to me. No matter how many times I tell myself I'm a good Dad, no matter how many times I tell myself I was a good Dad to

Adam, I'm not as sure of myself as I once was. Beth's character attacks arrive disguised as letters and legal motions from her attorney on a daily basis. Adam's vicious words cut like a surgeon's scalpel. His disgusting behavior breaks my heart into smaller pieces every day. I wouldn't blame anyone in my position for doubting himself a little bit. Third party validation is good medicine for a wounded ego – especially when that validation comes from the only person other than the alienating Mom and brainwashed child who has known me as "Dad."

November 8

I visited the Children's Visitation Center today. The Center could be an option as a neutral site for seeing Adam.

Vince, the Center's supervisor, explained that the Center's primary role is providing children with a safe, non-threatening environment to visit with their parents. Oh, I almost forgot something. Most of the parents who spend time with the children at the Center are convicted felons, child abusers and other potentially dangerous individuals. No matter what the crime, these people still have court-ordered rights to see their children, so Vince and his facility provide a valuable service.

All the parent-child visits at the Center are video and audio taped. Vince explained that judges often view the tapes before making final custody and visitation orders. An additional benefit, according to Vince, is the recording equipment keeps both the children and adults on their best behavior. And if the cameras don't motivate everyone to behave, the gun Vince wears on his hip usually does.

Vince finally got around to asking me why I contacted him. Most of his business, he said, comes directly from the court and attorneys. I explained my relationship with Adam and how we got to this point. I also told Vince about Beth's false abuse charges.

His cameras, I explained, would allow me to see my son and prevent Beth from saying I was physically abusive.

To say Vince was initially suspicious of me is an understatement. The tough guy said he would stop visitation at the first sign of trouble. Remembering Adam's fondness for hitting me, I responded that if he stopped visitation for the wrong reasons I would take my business elsewhere. The testosterone level in the room rose by the minute. Vince and I did everything but drop our pants, get out rulers and measure. But I guess Vince finally decided I wasn't very dangerous. When he got up from his desk to show me around the rest of the facility he threw his gun in a desk drawer.

November 9

I met face-to-face with Adam's domestic violence counselor today. Although we didn't cover any new ground I did bring him up to date on the plans for court-ordered visitation and the ongoing psychiatric evaluations.

Perhaps our biggest accomplishment was finally putting a face with the disembodied voice at the other end of the phone line. On second thought, that isn't much of an accomplishment. Adam's next appointment is in one week.

November 12

Despite the fact that we signed the form last week in court, Beth never gave Adam's school guidance counselor the permission slip so Adam could participate in the school's Divorce/Separation discussion group. I faxed the counselor a copy of the signed permission slip from my files. She faxed back a copy of Adam's report card. I am happy to report that the alienated child did not let his estranged relationship with me affect his grades – he received all A's for the first marking period of the sixth grade. I don't know if I should smile or cry. If Adam got bad grades I could at least tell myself that his poor performance in school is his subconscious way of saying he misses me.

I called my straight A student tonight. The conversation did not go well:

Mike:	I heard you had a good meeting with your attorney.
Adam:	How do you know? Did he tell you what I said?
Mike:	No, he didn't tell me what you said. He only told me you had a good meeting.
Mike:	(after a pause) Please don't hang up. Are you giving me your Hanukah list?
Adam:	I gave it to Mom to split up. You owe me $20 for my report card.
Mike:	Can I see your report card?
Adam:	I got all A's. There, are you happy?
Mike:	Can I see the report card? Do you think you could show it to me?
Mike:	(after a pause) Please don't hang up.
Adam:	Screw you.

Then I heard the click on the phone line that alerts me that the conversation ended.

Phil Crawford said he believed his client was coming around. He said Adam was "on board" with a visitation program. Adam isn't on board with anything. Either Adam was bullshitting his attorney or his attorney was bullshitting me. Maybe both.

November 25

Jared and I celebrated Thanksgiving with my family in Florida. Unfortunately, I was a little low on holiday spirit. I looked at the entire family sitting around the dinner table, but I only saw the one who was missing.

At one point during the day Jared was on the phone with Adam. I took the phone and wished my missing son a Happy Thanksgiving. Adam never said a word. He just put the phone down. Eventually, someone at his end hung it up.

November 29

The guidance counselor at Adam's school reported that Adam attended his first Divorce/Separation group meeting before the long Thanksgiving weekend. Adam was actually supposed to attend a meeting on November 16 but didn't come to school that day. The newest member of the group didn't say anything at the most recent meeting, but the counselor indicated he listened intently.

November 30

I had my first visit with Adam at the Visitation Center tonight. Overall, the two hours went better than Vince or I thought they would.

114

Adam talked quite a bit. He's angry about the divorce and my relationship with Kelly. He knows I see Kelly. In a sick twist worthy of a daytime soap opera, Beth and Kelly's ex-husband have become friends. I guess they compare notes on where the kids are and conclude if Kelly and I are both alone, we're together. Sometimes they're right. But right or wrong, Beth tells Adam I'm with Kelly.

Adam also told me I'm going through a "mid-life crisis." I asked him to define a mid-life crisis and he said, "It's when a guy your age buys a new car and new clothes because he thinks he is cool." The fact that I drove up in the same car I've driven for the last four years and wore a sweater and jeans Adam has seen me wear a hundred times did not lead Adam to rethink his diagnosis.

Adam gave Vince plenty of absurd reasons for his position. He said he doesn't want to see me because I was too strict when I lived in the house. Vince asked, "What's too strict?" Adam responded, "Dad never let me curse and Mom does." When Vince and I pressed Adam for further reasons for refusing to see me, Adam reminded me I once yelled at Jared for telling an insensitive joke about Hitler and the Jews. Adam also said I ate all the cookies in the house. I remember the Hitler incident and I plead guilty. However I'm innocent of the cookie consumption charges.

Vince surprised me. He was a good facilitator. Vince's obvious strengths are in the safety and peacekeeping departments. However he's done enough supervised visitation to pick up a few mediation skills. When I hit a wall with Adam, Vince stepped in and kept the dialogue moving.

December 1

I checked in with both the domestic violence counselor and the school guidance counselor today. The domestic violence counselor hasn't seen Adam in weeks. The guidance counselor reported that Adam attended his second Divorce/Separation group discussion the other day but still hasn't said anything.

From "Immaturity and Childish Central" – Beth refused to let me talk to Jared tonight. I called about 9:30 p.m. and she said, "I'm on the phone. You'll have to call back." Then she hung up. Her response isn't new – just standard operating procedure for Beth. But tonight she must have turned off the ringers because I kept calling back, and the phone just rang until 11:30 p.m. I finally got tired, gave up, and went to bed.

December 4

Vince was so encouraged by the progress we made with Adam last time that he tried taking us out to breakfast this morning. Breakfast was fine with me. From my perspective, Vince's presence is just as good as videotape for refuting abuse allegations.

Vince called Beth to work out the details but Beth said Adam had a Boy Scout outing and couldn't make it. Later I found out from Jared that Adam was home all morning. There was no Boy Scout outing. Beth made the whole thing up. Adam didn't even leave the house until Beth took him to a comic book store around 1:00 p.m.

December 6

What a difference one week makes. I had my second supervised visitation with Adam at the Visitation Center tonight. The two hours were brutal.

The night started with Adam refusing to enter the room where visits are supposed to take place. Adam wouldn't budge from the Center's lobby so Vince and I joined him there. We sat playing cards while Adam sat close by with his coat pulled over his head. Vince and I talked about Adam like he wasn't there – trying to get a reaction from him that could possibly end the stalemate. The only time Adam reacted was when I took his hand-held video game. My son wasn't pleased. He punched me for my transgression. Adam's inappropriate behavior brought Vince out of his chair and nose to nose with Adam's covered face. The tough guy told Adam he wasn't going to tolerate any of that behavior.

A few minutes later Adam went into a public bathroom outside the Center and refused to come out. Vince and I joined Adam, and the three of us spent the next 90 minutes in the men's room. Adam stayed locked in the bathroom stall while Vince and I took turns pacing past the urinal and sink.

Unfortunately, there is probably some sort of law about putting cameras in public bathrooms so Adam's performance is lost to future generations of parents interested in a first rate example of an alienated child's temper tantrum. For the most part, he cursed at us and called us names. He repeatedly gave us the finger. He threw toilet paper over the side of the bathroom stall. At one point Adam asked for a sharp object. He said he, "wanted to make himself bleed to death." When I asked him why he wanted to bleed to death he said, "Because you are torturing me, and I would rather be dead." Adam scratched his chest long enough with his fingernail to make a red mark and draw a little blood.

When Adam wasn't cursing or asking for sharp objects, he repeated words, phrases and ideas straight from Beth's mouth. Naturally, everything was negative and directed at me. At this point I can't remember exactly what he said. After my son said he would rather be dead than see me, the rest of the night just blurred together.

Vince is going to be busy tomorrow. He is calling all three attorneys and Dr. Stone, the psychologist doing the court-ordered evaluations. Vince realized he is in over his head with Adam. He wants Adam in therapy as quickly as possible.

December 7

I took Jared to see Dr. Stone today – the psychologist conducting the psychological evaluations. I really thought the evaluation process would include tests. You know, the patient looks at the inkblot and tells the doctor what he sees kind of stuff. But the psychologist explained he doesn't use tests, he gathers his information through interviews. Today was Jared's turn.

Dr. Stone asked Jared lots of questions – questions about Adam and questions about Jared's feelings about the divorce. The psychologist also asked Jared if Beth was responsible, either purposely or accidentally, of contributing to Adam's feelings towards me. Jared said yes, and explained how Beth talked negatively about me to keep Adam on "her side."

After he finished interviewing Jared, Dr. Stone disclosed he'd met with Beth once, but hadn't met Adam yet. I gave this man a retainer six weeks ago. I reminded him that even Vince recognized Adam needed therapy as soon as possible. He must finish up these evaluations so we can move on to the therapy, I said. In response he talked about his "banana" schedule and leaving phone messages for Beth. After everything I told him about Beth, did he think she'd call back in a timely manner? And what exactly is a banana schedule?

December 8

I checked in with Adam's school guidance counselor. He attended the Divorce/Separation group held two days ago. Adam listened but did not participate. The counselor might as well just record her message and send me the tape so I can play it once a week.

December 10

Adam and I met with Dr. Stone this afternoon. I guess after our last conversation the psychologist put a little more effort into getting hold of Beth.

Our time together seemed more like therapy than an evaluation to me. Having said that, the session went fairly well. Dr. Stone put the blame for Adam's anger at my feet. I didn't agree, but I went along with the professional and fell on my sword in front of Adam in the hope that an act of contrition would help Adam work through his anger.

One curious note – Dr. Stone told me privately that he knows Beth is happy with Adam's position and is not acting in his best interests. But he didn't address that issue during our 45-minute session.

As long as I had Adam's somewhat undivided attention, I asked him if he was going down to Florida over his Christmas break. My sister invited him to spend his break with her family. She would even pay for the plane ticket.

Adam said he wanted to go, but he would have to "ask Mom." I already knew from talking to Jill that Beth wasn't letting him go. Beth never technically said Adam couldn't go, but she never said he could go either. Instead, she just delayed giving Jill an answer until Jill lost the airline reservation she was holding in Adam's name.

Once again, Beth was more interested in disrupting Jared or Adam's relationship with my family than acting in Adam's best interest. Only this time she had added incentive. There was no way she would let Adam spend time with anyone who could possibly undo her good alienation work.

December 13

Beth was up to her old tricks with the phone this afternoon. She must have taken it off the hook. I tried calling Jared but all I got was a busy signal.

The telephone is an alienating parent's best friend. With all the services the phone company can provide – caller ID, call waiting, call blocking, call screening and voice mail – getting a busy signal or being on the other end of the line when someone hangs up on you is actually quaint and old fashioned. When Adam hangs up on me, at least he knows *I tried* talking to him. But Beth has a full complement of technology at her disposal. She can screen, block or ignore my calls, and Jared and Adam never even know I called.

December 15

Adam and I were supposed to meet with the good Dr. Stone today. But much like the second session at the Visitation Center fell apart after a good first visit, this second session with Dr. Stone fell apart before it even began.

When I arrived at the office, Dr. Stone reported that Adam refused to get in the car with Beth and come to our appointment. Instead of a bathroom, this time Adam found refuge in the woods behind the house.

The doctor and I both called Beth. My soon-to-be ex-wife hung up on me three times. She did accept Dr. Stone's calls. He encouraged her to get Adam in the car and bring him to the office – even if it meant we would only have a couple of minutes together.

But Beth and Adam never arrived. The last time Dr. Stone and Beth talked was about 90 minutes into our scheduled two-hour appointment. I listened in on the speaker phone.

By that time Adam was back in the house watching TV. Beth said she couldn't talk long because she was taking Adam to a Boy Scout Christmas party. Beth also told the doctor that Adam was sleeping over at a friend's tonight. Dr. Stone appeared frustrated when he hung up the phone. Surprisingly, the only reaction he gave me was a shrug of the shoulders and a "what are you going to do" look.

I didn't bother hiding my feelings. I was angry and asked the professional if he was going to include Beth's alienating behavior in his report to the court. After all, she not only defied a court order but also rewarded Adam's bad behavior with a party and sleepover. The only response I got from the doctor was, "There is no such thing as parent court."

Jared happened to be at the house for today's action. When I asked him if Beth tried getting Adam out of the woods and into the car, he said, "Mom didn't try too hard. She mostly talked on the phone."

December 18

Vince took his best shot at Beth and Adam today. He had as much success with them as Dr. Stone did the other day.

Beth was supposed to take Adam to the Visitation Center for our court-ordered time together. But here's a shocker – Beth called Vince and said she couldn't get Adam into the car. The tough guy wasn't deterred. Vince's attitude was that, if the alienated child refuses to come to the Center, the Center would go to the alienated child. Vince told me to meet him at the house. I waited outside while Vince went in.

121

Vince found Adam in bed sleeping. He tried waking Adam, and Adam kicked him. When Adam saw Vince wasn't scared away, Adam threatened to kill himself by wrapping my old jump rope around his neck. Vince still wasn't scared away. Vince calmly told Adam that at best, the jump rope is only good for a little rope burn and maybe passing out. Adam put the rope down.

Vince may have won the war of words, but Adam/Beth had the final word. Adam never left the house. Vince and I went to breakfast alone.

December 20

Today I argued with Lisa Slater, my attorney, over contempt motions.

Beth continues violating the judge's orders. She doesn't take Adam to therapy with Dr. Stone. She doesn't take Adam to Vince's Visitation Center. Beth is in contempt of court. It's that simple.

But Lisa is hesitant about filing a contempt motion and hauling Beth before the judge. My attorney thinks the psychologist's report documenting Beth's behavior will be more powerful without our appearing antagonistic. She also believes that at best, all the judge will do is slap Beth's wrist. So why bother?

How about because we're teaching Beth that she can disobey court orders and get away with it?

December 21

Tonight I spent time alone with my two sons for only the second time in five months. The last time we were together I took them to buy birthday presents for Beth. All I had to do was check the calendar to know why Adam was willing to see me tonight. There are only four shopping days left until Christmas. I imagine that Beth encouraged tonight's shopping expedition much more than she encouraged the recent failed court-ordered visits with Vince or Dr. Stone.

I told Adam the ground rules before we left – no hitting, cursing or rudeness. For the most part, we survived the two hours without incident. However Adam's attitude was disgusting. He only tolerated me because I drove him to the mall and paid for his present. Beth tried capitalizing on the situation by giving Adam the name of a jewelry store and a picture of the ring she told Adam she wanted for Christmas. When I told Adam I wasn't buying jewelry for him to give Mom, he picked out wind chimes instead.

I gave Adam a belated Hanukkah present before he got out of the car. I also told him that Jared would bring over the rest of his Hanukkah presents tomorrow morning. Adam's only response was to tell me he is not giving me anything for Hanukkah.

Adam's continuing behavior and attitude defies description. Beth the alienator has done an excellent job. Maybe my son is buried in this disgusting child somewhere. I don't know. After five months of experiences like tonight, I have a hard time believing that the Adam I loved exists anymore.

December 27

When I dropped Jared off at the house a few days ago I gave him more Hanukkah presents for Adam. I might as well have dropped everything into a black hole. Adam never acknowledged the gifts. He never called to say thank you.

I never heard from my son, but I did hear from his domestic violence counselor today. He called Beth last week but Beth said Adam didn't want an appointment. The counselor gave Beth an

123

open invitation to bring Adam in any time, but he didn't sound like he expected to continue as a player in this saga.

December 28

I met with Dr. Stone this afternoon – alone. Adam was scheduled to join us but Beth told Dr. Stone that Adam refused to attend, and she couldn't make him. She even tried justifying her non-actions by using Adam's jump rope threats with Vince last week as her reason for "keeping Adam home and safe."

Dr. Stone would only call Beth's actions "bad parenting."

December 29

Beth used her favorite weapon tonight – the telephone – in her never-ending attempts to disrupt my relationship with Jared.

I called Jared at 6:45 p.m. He was just sitting down to dinner and said he would call me by 7:15 p.m. When I didn't hear from him, I called back. The phone just rang. No one picked up. I didn't get through to Jared until 8:45 p.m. Jared said Beth was on the phone and wouldn't let him call me until she finished her conversation.

January 1

I picked Jared up at 6:30 a.m. in the middle of a blinding snowstorm. Just my luck – this morning the weather didn't cooperate any more than Beth ever does.

A storm is dumping snow across the entire Northeast. Meteorologists predicted the storm would start between 9:00 a.m.

and 12:00 p.m. and drop approximately one foot of snow on the area.

When I finally reached Jared last night, I asked him if I could pick him up at 11:00 p.m. or even 12:00 a.m. to avoid going out in this weather. Jared wanted to sleep here but Beth gave him a hard time because last night was "her night." Rather than fight with Beth, Jared said he would sleep at the house. We agreed I would pick him up by 9:30 a.m. – hopefully before the snow was too deep and the roads were too bad.

When I woke up at 6:00 a.m., snow already covered the ground. I tried calling Jared, but Beth must have turned off the ringers on the telephones. No one answered. I threw on some clothes and drove over to the house. I rang the doorbell until Jared answered the door. He dressed and we left.

Jared, despite his best efforts to stay neutral and above the fray, suffers when Beth refuses to co-parent. When we reached home, we talked about how hard it is for him to be in the middle of this mess. We talked about how Beth takes out her anger on Jared as a way to punish me. We covered a lot of ground.

At one point I asked Jared if there was anything I could do to make his life easier. He replied, "Yes, make Mom take responsibility for her actions." Unfortunately, Jared's request falls under the category, "easier said than done."

* * * *

Mike: What do you think of my strategy?

Dr. Davies: You mean looking for help from all those third parties – the domestic violence counselor, the school guidance counselor, the court-appointed attorney and psychological evaluator, even someone who runs a visitation center?

Mike: When you say it that way, it sounds like I involved too many people. But I wasn't about to leave a single stone unturned.

Dr. Davies: An alienated parent will go to any length to reconnect with his or her child. Let's face it – an alienated parent is a desperate parent. If you thought a psychic or magician could help reunite you with your son, you would call that person. The people you involved are excellent choices. An alienated parent must work within the legal and mental health systems.

Mike: What can anyone realistically expect from these people?

Dr. Davies: All you can expect from experts is that they act professionally, and even then you may be disappointed. Quite often an alienated parent expects psychologists and therapists to have special powers or expertise. The parent thinks, "This expert will evaluate my son properly. This other expert will fix my child's emotional problems. This third expert will reunite me with my child." But in reality the expert's power and expertise are limited by a couple of factors. If the alienating parent and child won't cooperate with the professional, there isn't much the professional can accomplish. If everyone were to cooperate with the professional, he or she would still be handicapped by the limitations of the mental health and legal systems.

Mike: What kind of limitations?

Dr. Davies: The biggest limitation is the inability to act quickly. Unless the professional can convince someone the child is in imminent danger, the legal and mental health communities move at an incredibly slow pace. When a child is in danger, the authorities move in quickly, evaluate the situation, and remove the child from the unsafe environment.

An alienated child is not typically seen as vulnerable to an immediate threat or harm. The child may suffer long-term emotional damage from living with an emotionally immature and controlling parent, but the child won't exhibit any obvious symptoms for a long time. Legal and mental health professionals only act quickly if they see scars or evidence. Plus, the alienating parent typically cooperates just enough with the professionals to leave them with the impression that he or she is trying to do her best for the child. The real goal is to limit their access to the child. But the more he or she appears to cooperate the fewer reasons the professionals have to act quickly.

Mike: You'd think Beth and Adam would at least cooperate with the domestic violence counselor – especially since they contacted him.

Dr. Davies: A domestic violence counselor wouldn't be my first choice to counsel a parental alienation family. An unaffiliated psychologist or therapist would be more appropriate. The unaffiliated professional enters a case without any preconceived ideas. A domestic violence counselor starts from a place where one parent is already assumed guilty of abusive behavior.

The counselor's mandate is to protect the rights and safety of children, and in the case of suspected child abuse, ensure the child isn't in any immediate danger. These counselors, even though they are predisposed to believe the victim's allegations, are very effective at evaluating alleged or potential victims of domestic violence. Not every person who visits a domestic violence center is a victim of domestic violence.

A physical or sexual abuse allegation presents an alienating parent with the perfect weapon. The alienating parent needs a good reason that he or she fights so hard to keep the other parent away from their child. The parent needs to convince him or herself, the child and anyone connected to the case that his or her actions are honorable and in the child's best interest. Despite the fact that the alienated parent had a normal, healthy relationship with the child before the divorce, the parent is hit with false abuse charges after the breakup of the marriage. The alienated parent who spanked his or her child must prove he or she didn't physically abuse the child. The alienated Dad who helped his young child at bath time must defend himself against allegations that he touched the child inappropriately. In your case you locked a door and blocked Adam from leaving a room. Whether you were within your rights to prevent Adam from leaving the room is irrelevant. Your actions led to charges that you are an abusive parent. False abuse charges are standard operating procedure in parental alienation cases. The alienating parent will make these claims to justify his or her actions, enlist a professional's support and validate his or her position. False abuse allegations are a very effective tool for furthering the alienating parent's cause.

Mike: How so?

Dr. Davies: Physical and sexual abuse is a big problem in our society. The alienating parent recites a very compelling story that starts, "My child and I were abused…." If the alienated child is older, can speak for him or herself, and corroborate the allegations, the counselor gives the charges even more weight. He or she becomes a very sympathetic listener. But if the allegations are false, the counselor will eventually identify a pattern that is not consistent with domestic violence. Domestic violence counselors are trained to address and evaluate false abuse claims.

Mike: What does the counselor look for?

Dr. Davies: Not so much what but whom. The counselor looks at everyone involved in the case. An abusive person typically won't cooperate with the counselor. The parent won't return phone calls or attend a meeting. A victim of false allegations will usually cooperate. An alienated parent falsely accused of abuse will most certainly cooperate, because the parent is desperately looking for anyone who can reunite him with his child.

The counselor also looks hard at the person making the allegations. After filing the initial complaint, did he or she substantiate the claims? Did he or she follow through with counseling for him or herself, or the child? An alienating parent is usually very convincing when he or she tells his or her story. But if the abuse allegations are false, the parent can't back up the story with factual information. Nor does the parent cooperate with counseling recommendations once he or she has the

professional's sympathy, support and validation.
The alienating parent and child's false allegations
are based on emotion, not reality. Their facts rarely
add up, and the claims fall apart very quickly. A
good clinician will uncover the truth. In your case,
Beth and Adam stopped cooperating with the
professional's recommendations for continued
counseling. The clinician should have recognized
that as a red flag indicating that the real issue was
about an unhealthy parent/child bond based on
manipulation and control rather than abuse at the
hand of the other parent.

Mike: I asked the court to appoint someone to do a
psychological evaluation in the hope that the
evaluation would lead to future counseling orders.
Is that a better idea?

Dr. Davies: A psychological evaluation is a much better
idea. But from what you've said you didn't get a
psychological evaluation. The evaluator in your
case did more of a psychosocial assessment. In a
psychosocial assessment the evaluator interviews
the family members and assesses the psychological
and social factors that are contributing to the current
situation. The purpose of this assessment is to make
a custody recommendation back to the court and
possibly even a recommendation for individual,
joint or family therapy.

Mike: How does an evaluator uncover factors like
poor object relations, unresolved abandonment
issues or borderline personality disorder through
interviews?

Dr. Davies: It's possible that someone will uncover
those factors in a psychosocial assessment. The

person conducting the interviews would need to be a very skilled clinician. He or she would typically conduct a series of 45-minute interviews and gather as much factual information as possible during the sessions.

A psychological evaluation is a much better tool for uncovering poor object relations, unresolved abandonment issues and other factors that lead to parental alienation. In this kind of evaluation, the psychologist performs a battery of personality and educational tests. These tests are similar to the tests schools use to determine a child's intellectual development and uncover learning disabilities or personality disorders. A good clinician performing a psychological evaluation will develop a complete picture of the dynamics contributing to a case of parental alienation.

A psychologist conducting a psychosocial assessment will only obtain what the person being interviewed is willing to provide. The psychologist must conduct very thorough interviews on the individual's family of origin and childhood issues to get past an alienating parent's rehearsed responses. Questions should cover everything from relationships with significant people – parents, brothers, sisters, aunts, uncles and cousins – to dependency issues. A trained evaluator doing a thorough evaluation can weed out the inconsistencies from the alienating parent's responses and get to an alienation diagnosis. A psychosocial assessment is not the most effective tool in this type of situation, but it can work.

Mike: How long should an evaluation take?

Dr. Davies: In a psychosocial evaluation, the evaluator should interview the child, alienating parent and alienated parent at least twice each. How quickly the psychologist recognizes the symptoms contributing to a case of parental alienation will depend on how much experience the psychologist has with alienation. But a psychologist could conduct the assessment I described in three weeks.

Mike: I think Dr. Stone forgot he was assessing the situation and was more interested in doing therapy. In fact, the first session we had with Adam went well. My first meeting with Adam at Vince's Visitation Center also went well. But both second sessions fell apart. Why?

Dr. Davies: Clearly both second sessions fell apart for one of two reasons – either the first sessions went too well for Adam, or they went too well for Beth. An inconsistent pattern like this is fairly common in alienation cases. Remember, the alienated parent and child operate on emotion.

If the sessions went too well for Adam, he was confronted with the reality that you're not the toxic person his mother has convinced him you are. Adam saw you're the same Dad he loved before Beth pulled him into the conflict. There was also a third party chipping away at Adam's defenses. Reality conflicted with his perceived reality. Without Beth around to refortify Adam's defenses, he felt very uncomfortable with his position. He may have even felt guilty about his position. When Adam told you in the bathroom that he felt tortured, he probably told you the truth. The only part Adam didn't understand was that the abusive, toxic father wasn't torturing him. Adam felt tortured because the reality of you as the loving father conflicted with the reality he must believe in order to survive. Rather than go through that again, Adam sabotaged the second sessions – either in person or by not showing up – in order to avoid the internal conflict.

That's one theory. The second theory is that the first sessions went too well for Beth. What do you think happened when Adam went home from the first sessions? Beth probably interrogated him about what happened and what was said. Beth put Adam back in an emotional bind. She probably even reminded Adam of her version of the truth and brought all Adam's anger front and center – effectively sabotaging any progress you might have made. I wasn't there, but I wouldn't be surprised if Beth's final message to Adam was, "Honey, you don't ever have to go back if you don't want to."

Mike: Adam was in real agony in the bathroom at the Visitation Center. Vince and I forced Adam to confront issues he didn't want to confront. Is forcing the issue like this really in the child's best interest? Did we run the risk of pushing Adam over the edge?

Dr. Davies: There really isn't a good time to crack the protective shell that an alienated child uses to protect himself. Adam had been living in a distorted reality for months. I believe the sooner you confront the child in a controlled setting, the better. A bathroom really isn't an optimum setting. An 11 or 12 year old doesn't have the coping skills to address his issues without the proper support. You ran the risk of pushing Adam to the point where he could have been a danger to himself or someone else. He

133

could have acted out at someone or acted inward due to his inner conflict.

When a child's belief system crumbles, the child needs something to fall back on. If everything the child believed has fallen apart, what's left? That's why the controlled setting is so important. Psychologists always make sure that no matter what happens with a patient during a session, by the end of the session the patient has had the opportunity to pull himself or herself back together. The patient must be healthy and safe when he or she walks out the door.

9

Potholes on the Road to Therapy

January 3

I TALKED WITH ADAM'S SCHOOL guidance counselor today.

Adam didn't attend today's Divorce/Separation program. When the counselor called Beth to enlist her help and support, Beth would only say, "It's probably best not to push him."

The counselor also reported that Adam didn't show up for the Divorce/Separation group right before the school's Christmas break. The guidance counselor sent someone to get Adam from the lunchroom, but Adam sent back the following message: "I'm not coming, and you can't make me."

The school and the guidance counselor are giving up. They won't use their usual repertoire of consequences – lower grades, detention or no recess – to compel Adam to attend the workshops. I wonder how the school would handle a student who refused to eat lunch in the cafeteria or wear shoes. Would the grown-ups abdicate the power to the child under those circumstances?

I left the school and picked up Jared. After our conversation about Beth taking out her anger on him, I decided Jared could benefit from some therapy. Jared was so upset over the incident that he didn't object.

I prepped Dr. Stone before arriving. Even so he kept blurring the line between evaluating the situation for his report and counseling Jared. At one point I asked Jared to leave the room so I could tell Dr. Stone that if he didn't make therapy his main focus, I would take Jared somewhere else.

Then I left them alone for the last 30 minutes of the session. I don't know what they discussed, but Jared was in a good mood and talkative on the ride home.

January 4

Adam had an appointment scheduled with Phil Crawford, the attorney for the minor children, after school. But during a school-day meeting with the guidance counselor, Adam talked about suicide. I'm not sure if Adam was making a new threat to get out of his appointment with his attorney or talking about his previous threat to Vince. In any event, the counselor became alarmed and called Beth and Mr. Crawford.

The attorney met Beth at the school to personally take Adam to see Dr. Stone. Adam saw his attorney and made a run for it across a muddy football field. Mr. Crawford took off through the mud after him – $200 shoes and all – and eventually got Adam in the car and to Dr. Stone's office.

The two attorneys and the psychologist – Lisa, Mr. Crawford and Dr. Stone – advised me to stay away from the meeting, so I did. Dr. Stone called me afterwards and said that he doesn't think Adam is suicidal. No kidding.

Mr. Crawford wants to appoint a Guardian Ad Litem (GAL) for Adam. Unlike an attorney for a minor child, who can only represent to the court what the child wants, a GAL represents to the court what he or she thinks is in the child's best interest.

The topic of a GAL came up among Mr. Crawford, Dr. Stone and Beth. Adam's attorney indicated that Beth said she might oppose the GAL because she doesn't think a GAL "is in Adam's best interest."

January 5

Dr. Stone called tonight and said that he doesn't recommend a GAL at this time. He said Beth is ready to co-parent with me and set a good example for Adam. Dr. Stone wants to work with us and pursue this strategy first.

This strategy is off the mark and I told him so. What the psychologist doesn't recognize is that Beth will say all the right things in front of him ("Of course I want Adam to have a good relationship with Mike"), then go home and reinforce Adam's already entrenched position. ("Your father called me more names tonight.")

The professional may have more experience in psychology than I do, but I have more experience with Beth than he does. Unfortunately, my experience doesn't count for much in court. Lisa believes the judge won't appoint a GAL without Stone's support. For now, the GAL issue is dead.

January 6

So Dr. Stone thinks Beth is ready to co-parent with me? He must be practicing in *The Twilight Zone*. Case in point:

When Beth called Jared tonight, I told Jared he shouldn't hang up without giving me the phone. When Jared told Beth I needed to talk to her, Beth replied, "I have to go to the bathroom." Jared asked Beth to call me back in five minutes.

After fifteen minutes, I hadn't heard from her. I tried calling, but couldn't get through. Beth had turned the answering machine on. I left a message, but Beth never called back.

January 13

Beth wants me to give her an additional $100 so Adam can go on a camping trip with a new backpack. I don't have the money. Beth's refusal to get a real job, i.e., a job that could potentially lower her future alimony and child support, is killing us. Of course, Adam doesn't know the truth about our financial situation. He only knows I work and make money and Beth doesn't.

Here's the Catch-22 of being an alienated parent:

If I had the money and paid for the trip and backpack, Adam would never say thank you or even tell me anything about the trip. I'd just reinforce his belief that Dad is an ATM and doesn't deserve even the smallest courtesy. But if I don't pay for the trip, Beth will tell Adam that I don't care enough about him to pay for his activity. She'd probably also throw in that I'm out spending the money on my girlfriend instead of on him.

Since I don't have the money, the point is moot. I'm forced to take the parental alienation behind door number two.

January 17

Dr. Stone called today and said Beth wanted to bring Adam into his office to meet with me. When I picked up Jared this afternoon, I had the chance to ask Adam how he felt about getting together:

Mike:	Did you tell Dr. Stone you want to meet with me?
Adam:	No.
Mike:	Did you tell Mom to tell Dr. Stone you want to meet with me?
Adam:	No.
Mike:	Are you interested in meeting with Dr. Stone and me?
Adam:	No.
Mike:	Would you like to get together with me without Dr. Stone?
Adam:	No.

January 21

Dr. Stone left me a voice mail this evening. He said he met with Beth and Adam the other day and would like to set up a meeting with Adam and me.

__January 28__

Dr. Stone and I have been playing phone tag for an entire week. The professional has a knack for calling me where I'm not. If I'm at work during the day, he calls the house. If I'm at home in the evening, he calls the office or my cell phone. He probably thinks leaving messages rather than having conversations is a good communication skill.

When we finally connected tonight, he had forgotten last week's voice mail about a meeting with Adam. Now he's back to his old idea about meeting with Beth. Dr. Stone thinks that if Adam knew Beth talked to me, he'd know its okay for him to talk to me. Of course, Stone is operating on the assumption that Beth will deliver the message. I'm not making any such assumption.

__January 31__

I had the big meeting with Beth and Dr. Stone today.

Beth kept saying she wants Adam to have a relationship with me, and she has never done anything to undermine our relationship. According to Beth, my problems with Adam are my own fault. She even told Stone that she couldn't be devious with Adam, because she is not a devious person. I laughed so hard that Dr. Stone scolded me like a teacher scolding a student for fooling around in class.

However, the court-appointed psychologist might have gotten through to her with one simple comment. "I can't recommend joint custody if you two don't start communicating about the kids," he said. Presto – in the last 12 hours Beth called twice to talk about Adam. He's at home sick. She even invited me into the house to see him.

Whatever bug Adam had, he still had enough strength to kick and punch me when I came into the house. I asked if I could take him out to dinner for his birthday in a few weeks. He said no. Then I told him I loved and missed him and that I hoped he felt better. That was pretty much it.

February 1

Beth's cooperation as it related to Adam lasted approximately 24 hours.

I asked her if I could come by and see Adam today, and she said no. I asked to talk to Adam. She handed him the phone; he handed it right back to her. When I asked her what she was going to do about Adam's refusal to talk to me, she said, "He's sick. I can't punish him when he is sick."

February 3

I called and asked Beth to put Adam on the phone. She handed him the phone, and he handed it right back to her. Once again I asked Beth what she planned on doing about Adam's refusal to talk to me. She said, "I'll handle it." I asked her twice how she planned on "handling it" but she refused to provide details.

Beth won't do anything. She just loves jerking me around.

February 11

Dr. Stone's big strategy is falling apart fast. Beth refuses to talk to me about the kids. Adam refuses to talk to me about anything. He's hung up on me at least once a day for the last week.

February 21

Adam's birthday is tomorrow. He came to the door tonight to take his gifts but was very rude. He said he wouldn't talk to me if I called tomorrow to wish him a happy birthday. He wouldn't go out to dinner with me. I finally asked him if he could say thank you for his gifts. He responded, "You don't deserve a thank you."

February 22

My son turned 12 today. I called to wish him a happy birthday, but he wouldn't come to the phone.

Later, Beth called and invited me over. When I arrived Adam heard me coming and ran downstairs to the basement. I talked to him from the top of the steps for a minute (he didn't respond) and then left.

February 27

Beth is back to her old tricks with the telephone.

I called Jared at 8:35 p.m. Beth said she was on the phone, and she would have him call me back. I never heard from Jared. I called back at 10:20 p.m. I asked him why he hadn't called. He said Beth never gave him the message. While we were on the phone, Beth kept yelling at Jared to get off the phone because she had to make a call.

I called back at 11:00 p.m. Adam picked up the phone, heard my voice and hung up.

March 1

I met with Dr. Stone today. We agreed that Adam would remain firmly entrenched in his current position until he reaches puberty and/or Beth is involved with someone. At that point, Adam's need to identify with Dad rather than Mom, combined with Beth's focus on a new relationship, might be enough to release Adam from Beth's emotional bondage.

Dr. Stone also isn't ready to release this case into the hands of the court-appointed psychologist. He wants to stay involved. What does it matter? Beth and Adam will blow off appointments with the new doctor as easily as they blow off appointments with this one. And get away with it too.

March 6

When Adam hung up on me tonight, it bothered me more than usual. Perhaps it had something to do with the fact that Jared and I watched a movie this evening – *He Got Game* with Denzel Washington and Ray Allen. I thought the movie was about basketball. The movie was really about the estranged relationship between a father and son. The son didn't want the father in his life.

Some days movies are an escape from reality. Other days movies reflect reality. On this day *He Got Game* hit too close to home for me.

March 7

I called Jared from 10:20 p.m. to 11:00 p.m. Nobody picked up the phone. I was forced to choose from one of the following possible conclusions:

- Beth is on the phone and refuses to use the call waiting because she knows I'm calling.

- Jared doesn't hear the phone ringing. Beth and/or Adam do hear it ringing, but don't answer because they know I'm calling.

- No one is home. One of the kids got hurt and everyone rushed to the emergency room.

I knew my first conclusion was probably correct. However, the last scenario sat in my stomach until I finally got through to Jared about 11:05 p.m. I should buy Jared a pager. Then if I paged him and didn't hear from him I'd only be wondering if the batteries went dead or he left it somewhere.

March 19

At Beth's invitation, I went over to the house to try talking to Adam. However before I arrived, Beth hit me with her new ground rules:

- I am not to sit down on a couch and "make myself comfortable."

- If Adam runs downstairs, I am not to follow him. I must talk to him from the top of the steps.

When Adam saw me, he ran down into the basement and locked himself in the bathroom. Despite Beth's rule, I followed Adam downstairs and talked to him through the door for a minute. Then I stopped talking and moved away. Adam came out, saw me standing across the room and literally jumped back in the bathroom. He acted like I had some highly contagious disease, and he couldn't breathe the same air I breathed without being infected.

I talked to Adam through the door for another minute and left. My son never said a word.

As I was walking out the door Beth casually mentioned that Adam and his friend had an argument in school yesterday, one of them said something about a gun, and both kids lost recess privileges for a few days. Everything is under control, she said.

PS – I didn't sit on the couch.

March 21

Everything is not under control at Adam's school. The school principal indicated the gun reference was much more serious, and had a much bigger history, than Beth indicated.

It seems Adam's friend was sleeping over a couple of weeks ago and the two kids argued. The argument escalated and Adam ended up on top of the other boy, choking him. The boy bit Adam in retaliation.

Over the last two weeks, Adam and his friend have been "dissing" each other in school. "Dissing" is short for disrespecting. Last week, according to the principal, Adam "goaded" the other kid into the gun reference:

Adam: You can't beat me up. You'd have to bring a gun to do anything to me.

Kid: Maybe I will bring a gun.

Another student heard this exchange and told a teacher.

After meeting with Adam, Beth, the school superintendent and the guidance counselor, the principal decided not to suspend Adam. Instead, Adam will be required to spend one week (during recess and after school) in the school's anger management counseling program. The principal said he told Beth that Adam needs serious counseling. Adam, according to the principal, thinks he is smarter than everyone and doesn't have to listen to anyone – he can do what he wants without consequences. When Beth told the principal that she can't get Adam into counseling he supposedly responded, "Who's the parent, and who's the child?" I seriously doubt the school will allow Adam to skip this program.

March 25

Both Adam's guidance counselor and the school's principal gave me positive feedback on my son's participation in the anger management counseling. They believe Adam is much more aware of the consequence of his words and actions and, they believe, he won't make the same mistake again.

I asked the Guidance Counselor if she thinks Adam's experience in school would translate into anything positive in other areas of his life. She couldn't answer me. In fairness, parental alienation is way beyond her scope or expertise.

April 1

I think I have the answer to the question I asked the Guidance Counselor the other day – no.

AOL sent me a report concerning a "Terms of Service" violation. It seems Adam was on the computer and sent an instant message with the phrase "fuck you" in it. The recipient of Adam's message didn't appreciate it and reported Adam to AOL.

I tried discussing this situation with Beth. First she admitted Adam was on the computer. But after I told her what happened, she said Adam wasn't on the computer. Beth then accused me of having his password and trying to make Adam look bad.

I sent Adam an email about his language but that's as close as I got to him today. When I made my nightly call, Adam refused to come to the phone.

April 4

It was a big day in court today. Dr. Stone made an appearance.

Dr. Stone once again proved what a horrendous choice he was for an evaluator. I don't make many mistakes, but when I do the mistakes are usually big ones. Selecting Dr. Stone to do the psychological evaluation was the mother of all mistakes.

In the course of two hours he made three different recommendations concerning Adam. Each recommendation was designed to placate whomever he was talking to at the moment.

At one point I thought Adam was going to be admitted to a hospital for in-patient evaluation and therapy. Mr. Crawford, the court's family relation counselor, and Dr. Stone (we thought) all agreed that this was the best course of action. I also agreed. Naturally, Beth and her attorney opposed the move.

But then Dr. Stone left the building. Once he was away from everyone, he talked by phone with Mr. Crawford and backed off his original recommendation. He told the attorney that he wouldn't recommend in-patient treatment, but he wouldn't oppose it either.

That was all Beth's attorney needed to hear. She called Dr. Stone next. For his newest audience the doctor said that he definitely opposed in-patient therapy – giving Beth all the ammunition she needed to succeed in fighting off this course of action.

The best thing to come out of today's conference was that Dr. Stone is out of the game. He has two weeks to submit his written evaluation. He will not do any more therapy or facilitation. We're moving on to someone else.

In court Beth was so upset when it looked like Adam was going to be hospitalized, that she asked me to come by the house and see him. So on the way home, I called to see if I was still invited. Here's a shocker – I was no longer invited.

Beth's change of heart didn't surprise me, but Adam's response to my nightly call did. Rather than just hang up on me or call Jared to the phone he said, "Fuck you."

That's the first time Adam said that in a while. Since my son seemed to be in a verbal mood I asked why he needed to talk that way. Adam wouldn't answer me. He just kept shouting that I should stop harassing him and violating his rights.

I challenged him – "You keep telling people you're so mature. Prove it and talk normally without cursing or hanging up." That approach didn't work. Nothing worked. But I do give Adam credit for getting off one good line:

He reminded me that I used to say that while he lives under my roof he lives by my rules. Adam said he doesn't live in my house anymore, so he doesn't have to follow my rules.

Of course I responded. But I'll be damned if I remember what I said. It's been a long day.

April 9

I'm tired of waiting for Dr. Stone's evaluation. I'm tired of waiting for Phil Crawford to return a call. I'm tired of waiting for Lisa to file contempt motions and for the judge to rule on them. I exercised my court-ordered right to parenting time with Adam today.

The other day I put everyone on notice that I wasn't taking no for an answer. My insistence generated a flurry of phone calls, emails and letters, all at approximately $250 an hour, among the attorneys. At least when I arrived at the house at the appointed time, Adam got in the car. Jared got in the car too. Jared calls today and tomorrow, "Dad Days."

Adam climbed in with his headset over his ears and his hat pulled down over his eyes. He was a real beauty on the ride to the amusement center – cursing, kicking the back of the seats, playing with the car door handle, and trying to rip up a road atlas he found under the seat.

At one point I looked in my rear view mirror and saw Beth following us – another direct violation of the court's orders and her latest strategy to undermine my position as a responsible parent. Jared saw Beth too and asked why she was following us. My 12-year-old son, who hadn't said anything except curse words up to that point, started clarifying for his older brother what he agreed to as it related to our time together. I tried setting Adam straight about the court order and his "rights," but I would have had more success hitting my head against a wall.

When we arrived at the amusement center, Adam wrapped dental floss around his neck and around the little hook over the car door. I had to use Jared's Swiss Army mini-scissors to cut Adam free.

Once inside, Jared and Adam started playing this big video game that could accommodate four players at once. I watched the kids play for a little while and then decided to join them. I positioned myself between Jared and Adam and dropped in my token. For the next hour, the three of us played this game –working together to beat the various dragons and demons on the screen.

Adam acted okay. He answered my questions about how I should play the game. He didn't act like I had a highly contagious disease that he would catch just by standing next to me. Once or twice he asked nicely for additional tokens. When a huge dragon devoured my character I screamed "No!" Even Adam laughed.

After about an hour we were out of tokens and out of time. On the way out, Adam asked me if I would buy him some pizza. I gave him a choice of eating at a table or taking the pizza in the car. He chose the table and Jared and I sat sipping sodas while Adam ate.

By the time Adam finished eating, we were running late. Since Beth was sitting outside, I told Adam he could drive home with Mom if he wanted. He literally ran to her car. Jared and I headed in a different direction to visit with friends in Connecticut.

All in all, not a bad first step. But our first meeting at Vince's center and our first appointment with Dr. Stone went well too.

April 10

Jared left his backpack at Beth's yesterday. After calling Beth to make sure the backpack was there, he asked me to drive him over to pick it up.

When we arrived, I asked Beth to send Adam to the door. I wanted to return the CD player he left in my car yesterday. Beth refused to send Adam to the outside garage door or let me come up to the inside door. Instead, Beth told Jared she would ground him if he didn't bring in Adam's things.

Oh yea – I'm back to status quo with Adam. Despite our somewhat positive experience yesterday, he hung up on me when I called him tonight.

April 16

Adam is predictable if nothing else.

Our second attempt to spend some time together went as poorly as our second visits (or attempted visits) at Vince's center and Dr. Stone's office.

This time Adam drove to the amusement center with Beth. When he got out of her car, he cursed me and kicked my car. Then he kicked and punched me. Then he ran away.

Twenty minutes later I found Adam in Beth's car. They were ready to leave. Despite Lisa's strongly worded letters and phone calls about Beth's attempt to insert herself into my time with Adam during the last visit, she stayed at the amusement center. I pointed out to Beth that she couldn't leave – my time with Adam wasn't up yet. She left anyway.

Jared witnessed the entire disgusting episode and summed up everything best. "It's too early in the morning for this," he said.

April 18

My attorney notified Beth (through her attorney) that I was exercising my right to parenting time with Adam tonight. I planned on picking up Jared and Adam at 6:30 p.m. and taking them out to dinner.

Well, planned may be too strong a word. I was so sure Adam wouldn't come with us that before I left the house this morning I took something out of the freezer to cook when Jared and I got home.

Beth and Adam weren't even home when I arrived at the house. Jared and I ate at home.

April 19

Another day in court; another day we didn't accomplish anything.

Beth has another new lawyer (her third). He sent my attorney a letter at 4:30 p.m. yesterday afternoon and said he couldn't appear in court for today's status conference because he was involved in a trial. One attorney can't unilaterally cancel a court-ordered status conference, so Lisa and I showed up when we were supposed to. Two hours later the judge said he wouldn't move forward without Beth's new counsel. He scheduled another status conference for May 8 to cover the same ground we were supposed to cover today.

Feeling a bit depressed from the non-events of the last two days, I asked Jared what he would think of me if I left Adam alone and basically said, "I'm done. Call me when you want to see me."

Jared said he wouldn't think less of me for doing that, but he also said he didn't think it would be a good idea. Jared thinks Adam needs, "a good mediator – someone like Dr. Stone but better."

Perhaps that good mediator will be Dr. Jack Harris. Dr. Harris is Adam's new court-appointed psychologist. He's supposed to be one of the best parental alienation professionals in the state. Adam's first appointment with Dr. Harris is next week.

April 20

Lisa tried setting up my weekly time with Adam through Beth's new attorney. The guy didn't even return her calls or respond to her letters. I hope the judge will hear my contempt motions soon.

April 26

Both Lisa and I tried setting up parenting time with Adam for tomorrow night. Once again Beth's new lawyer did not return my attorney's call. Beth told me Adam did not want to go. The judge will hear my contempt motion next week.

April 30

Well, what do I know? Not much it seems. The judge did not hear my contempt motion today.

First, Beth's new lawyer showed up one hour late. Then the judge closed the courtroom to hear testimony in a closed case. At 2:00 p.m. Beth's new lawyer wanted to put all motions off until a status conference on May 8. He wasn't prepared. We said no. But by the time we went before the judge it was 3:10 p.m. The judge was leaving at 4:00 p.m. and had two other cases to hear. So the judge put everything off until May 8.

Today was the second time Beth's new lawyer wasted everyone's time and money. However, Lisa and I sat in the sun and had a nice chat about exercise. Our conversation cost me $250. The rest of this wasted day cost me a lot more.

May 3

Adam's school called. They asked me to come in and meet with his teacher and guidance counselor because Adam's academic performance is dropping off.

Adam hands in assignments late, if at all. He had six weeks to do a report on Greece and turned in something that looked as if he threw it together at the last minute. His teacher rewarded him with an F. When the guidance counselor questioned Adam about his lack of effort, the former straight-A student said he didn't care.

Everyone was also concerned about a comment Adam made to his guidance counselor. The counselor pointed out to Adam that he could get ink poisoning from writing on his arm. Adam responded, "I don't care if I live or die."

We talked for about 45 minutes – mostly about how to change Adam's attitude as it relates to his work. We also talked about keeping the lines of communication open between the school and Dr. Harris, Adam's new therapist.

On the way out of the building I passed Adam coming in from gym. I smiled and waved. Adam looked the other way.

May 7

In the last few weeks Dr. Harris met with Beth and me individually. He also met once or twice with Adam. Today Dr. Harris decided to go for broke – a meeting with Adam and me.

When I arrived, Dr. Harris explained he wanted to try something different. We were all going to sit quietly in the same space for 35 minutes without talking. Dr. Harris wanted to show Adam we could all agree on something, even if that something was nothing.

Sitting in Dr. Harris's office with only my thoughts to pass the time, I couldn't decide if I was in the middle of a *Seinfeld* episode or a 1970s encounter group minus the incense and ugly clothes. Since I didn't find anything funny about the experience, I decided on the encounter group. We all got through it. I even managed to stay awake – no small trick considering the office was very hot and the couch was very comfortable.

Dr. Harris thought we took a good first step. Maybe he is right. Even though Adam punched me in the stomach on his way out the door, I could tell his heart really wasn't in it.

May 8

Dr. Stone was back in court today to provide his evaluation – seven months after the judge ordered it and one month after the judge gave him two weeks to produce a written document. I guess his "banana" schedule prevented him from writing an evaluation. I know the threat of a subpoena prevented him from taking any more time. So instead of a written report, we got the doctor in the flesh.

Dr. Stone entered the courtroom and said hello to both Beth and me. Then he announced that he was sitting as far away from both of us as possible in order to maintain his neutrality. Isn't an evaluation supposed to be an objective report and not some exercise in fence straddling? I had the feeling that Stone's misguided sense of the evaluator's role was about to reach its apex.

Mr. Crawford, who became Adam and Jared's Guardian Ad Litem a few weeks ago, conducted Dr. Stone's examination on the witness stand. After qualifying Stone as an expert, the GAL wasted no time in asking him his opinion of Adam. The newly qualified expert wasted no time in describing Adam as daring and rebellious, and his position as, *"aligned with his mother against his father ... in ways that are similar to what is referred to in the literature as Parental Alienation Syndrome."* However, Dr. Stone also said that

155

Adam's position, *"Goes way beyond what the mother herself articulates as wanting... although I think there are some unconscious forces that have been created in the family that get communicated in one way or another that give this boy the message that his mother needs his support and loyalty."*

Dr. Stone also delivered his interpretation of Dr. Richard Gardner's, author of *The Parental Alienation Syndrome*, recommendation for dealing with severe parental alienation cases and why he believes that approach is inappropriate in this situation:

"It might be advisable in cases of very severe parental alienation to actually remove the child from the care of the parent who he's close to and compel that child to reside with the parent he won't deal with. I think this is an inappropriate solution in this case. I think there is reason to believe that, over time, because there was a quality relationship between father and son in the past, that the relationship can be rebuilt once the divorce is settled and if therapy continues."

After a follow-up question from the GAL on why compelling the child to reside with the parent he won't deal with is an inappropriate solution given the facts of this case, Dr. Stone continued:

"First of all even Dr. Gardner recommends that radical solution only in the most severe cases of parental alienation. And these include cases where there is absolutely no relationship whatsoever between the two parents. Where there are all sorts of false or exaggerated allegations of abuse. And where the child steadfastly insists on no relationship whatsoever. These are very extreme cases. I would see this case as more in the moderate range rather than the severe range. And even Dr. Gardner doesn't advocate that radical type of solution in the moderate cases."

On cross-examination, my attorney went after Dr. Stone on his characterization of my situation as only "moderate parental alienation." She pointed out that Adam refuses to have any relationship with me. Dr. Stone had a different take on our relationship:

There is some relationship between Adam and his father. For example, Adam is very comfortable giving his father a shopping list and telling him what presents he'd like for his birthday or Hanukkah. He has a utilitarian approach to his father at the moment.... Every once in a while, they'll talk briefly on the phone. The conversations have not typically, in recent months, been very polite or very protracted. But there has been some discussion periodically."

Dr. Stone called parental alienation a "family dynamic," but refused to come down hard on Beth for her role in this family's dynamics. During cross-examination Lisa asked if Beth's behavior sent Adam certain messages that led to the alienation:

"Well it certainly can be contributory to a parental alienation dynamic. It's not at all unusual in the process of a contested divorce for children to hear one parent say negative things about the other parent. And most divorce agreements I see contain wording that reminds parents that they should speak respectfully about each other or not say anything at all about each other, if they can only say negative things. Parents often need these reminders because emotions run high and there is, obviously, a lot of hurt and anger floating around. Kids pick up these messages. I don't believe I've seen evidence that Adam has been explicitly told not to see his father. It's more a kind of passive inability to compel him to fulfill his obligation to talk to his father and visit him that I have observed."

When Lisa followed up and asked Dr. Stone to explain how an alienating parent specifically alienates the child from a parent, he let Beth off the hook again:

Well, I can speak somewhat generically, and I'm not absolutely certain that these kind of things happened in this particular case. But typically, the parent who Gardner would describe as alienating would make comments about the other parent, in this case the father; that make it clear to the child that this is a man who deserves to be punished. That he abandoned us or left us with a lot of expenses. Or he's cheated on us because he's got another girlfriend. And the child picks up these messages as a request for loyalty and aid. Sometimes it gets conveyed a little more directly. Like the mother might be crying and say, 'Come here. I need a hug.' Or, 'I'm lonely.' And the child might feel with just a few of these incidents that it's his place to provide comfort and care to a mother who's been hurt by the father. There are sometimes even more indirect things; for example, a child may overhear a mother's conversation to a friend or a relative on the phone, talking about her outrage at the estranged husband's behavior. And the child picks up these messages, not being relayed directly to him, but just overhearing them, and has a kind of indirect invitation to be on the side of that hurt parent... so these are some of the kind of indirect messages that kids pick up. And I think Adam has been particularly vulnerable to them.

Attorney Slater tried one more time to get Dr. Stone to draw a direct link from Beth to alienating behavior and succeeded. After the judge overruled Beth's attorney's objection to attributing the behavior Dr. Stone described to Beth, the psychologist responded:

If I recall the question accurately, you were asking me if I feel that there was alienating behavior of the covert type in this case. And I would have to say 'yes,' I do believe that there was.

But that's as much as we got from Dr. Neutrality. Beth's attorney didn't ask Dr. Stone any questions about parental alienation, Adam, Beth or me. In fact, Beth's newest legal representative only asked Dr. Stone if he were going to provide a written report and if he would charge for writing that report. Given his testimony, Stone said he saw no reason to write a report; but yes he would charge extra if the court wanted one. The judge saw no reason Dr. Stone should write a report either.

A few things struck me as odd about Dr. Stone's testimony – and ultimately, his role as the evaluator.

The first thing that bothered me was that Dr. Stone represented a number of "facts" to the court that he just plain had wrong. Some facts were important. He characterized my relationship with Adam as moderate parental alienation, ignored Beth's false abuse claims, and downplayed her impact as the alienating parent. Other facts, such as mistakes in dates or time frames, were insignificant.

In his defense, Dr. Stone had multiple people telling him different versions of the same story. And he testified without notes on events that occurred months before. However I expected the court to give Dr. Stone's testimony a lot of weight. After all, the court-appointed psychologist represented the only independent, objective person involved in this case. I would think that any person in Dr. Stone's role would make sure what he or she said was correct – right down to the smallest detail. But Dr. Stone's testimony contained many inaccuracies – inaccuracies that he authoritatively represented to the court as truths.

I was angry when Dr. Stone's misinformation hurt my case and quite pleased when it made Beth look bad. But I took little comfort in the fact that Dr. Stone misrepresented plenty of facts on both sides of the case. It's true that whatever damage he did to one side was balanced by the damage he did to the other side. However since Adam's future was at stake, I had no tolerance for any mistakes. Ultimately, the only person damaged by Dr. Stone's errors was Adam.

The second thing that bothered me was the professional's willingness to accept Adam's stated position at face value and blame him for his decisions. Adam is only 12 years old. Yet Dr. Stone discussed Adam's comments as if this 12 year old was an independent thinker and decision maker who just didn't happen to have the legal right to make decisions that his father disagreed with. The doctor did not discuss the emotional conflict and inner turmoil that any child in Adam's position experiences when pressured to stay loyal to one parent at the expense of his or her healthy relationship with the other previously loved parent. My emotionally troubled youngster would have been better served if Dr. Stone repeated less of what he said and explained more of what a child in Adam's position typically feels and thinks.

Finally, my biggest problem with Dr. Stone's testimony was his misguided sense of the evaluator's role and his neutral approach to this case.

Dr. Stone's testimony reminded me of the algebra proofs the math teacher required us to do in high school. Here's how the algebra assignments worked: the teacher gave the class the answer to the equation, and the class was required to outline the mathematical steps that proved the answer was correct.

The neutral Dr. Stone's answer to this parental alienation equation was that Beth and I share joint legal custody of Jared and Adam, and physical custody of Jared. Dr. Stone's answer also included therapy for Adam, and ultimately, a shared parenting situation where Adam followed Jared's schedule and spent equal amounts of time with both parents.

Dr. Stone's answer was fine. The Guardian Ad Litem and I shared his views on custody. Beth said, up to this point, that she also supported the shared custody arrangement. But much like an algebra student, Dr. Stone started with his answer, and then used his testimony to prove to the judge that his answer was correct. His approach may have taken him to the correct response, but his route left Adam in the dust.

In order to arrive at shared custody, Dr. Stone couldn't appear to favor one side over the other. He stayed neutral – ignoring Beth's overt actions but parroting her self-serving comments indicating that Adam and I should have a relationship. Rather than hold Beth accountable for sending Adam the wrong messages about me, he blamed Adam for perceiving the wrong messages from his mother. Dr. Stone couldn't be too negative about Beth because if he did, his custody recommendation wouldn't stand up. Everything Dr. Stone said was calculated to support, or at least not jeopardize, his opinion on custody.

I wasn't looking for Dr. Stone to recommend I have full custody of Jared and Adam, but I was looking for him to recognize clearly Beth's alienating behavior and paint the judge a picture that showed Beth purposely not acting in her child's best interests. The incentive Beth needs to stop her alienating and destructive behavior can only come from a judge willing to punish her for her actions. Instead the doctor painted the judge a picture with enough ambiguity and shades of gray to leave the judge with doubts about Beth's role and intentions. According to Dr. Stone, bad parenting is not a crime. Violating court orders is. However, by shifting the responsibility for Adam's behavior away from Beth and towards Adam, Stone may have planted an interesting question or two in the judge's mind: "Is punishing an ineffective parent for violating court orders punishing the right person? Furthermore, will the punishment even work?"

After the Dr. Stone's testimony and a break for lunch, Beth showed her true colors. Her new attorney informed us that the parenting agreement with the shared custody language is history. Lisa, Phil Crawford, and Beth's former attorney worked hours to draft the agreement. Beth couldn't even wait for Dr. Stone's chair to get cold before reversing her previously agreed to position. Because of, or maybe in spite of, the professional's testimony, Beth now wants full legal custody of both Jared and Adam. She wants to do away with Jared's schedule and take away all his time with me. Naturally, she doesn't think Adam ever needs therapy or that he should spend any time with me. When I wouldn't agree to her new demands, the judge ordered the trial to begin on May 23.

Before we left, my attorney once again asked the judge to rule on my contempt motions against Beth and once again his honor refused. He said he would hear my motions during the trial. And then for effect he added, *"If someone is in contempt of court, they'll have to answer to me for that. Because as I've expressed many times, I take a very dim view of people who violate court orders and that includes automatic orders of the court. The whole system collapses when people violate court orders."*

May 21

I met with Adam and Dr. Harris twice more in the last couple of weeks. Adam behaved progressively worse at each visit – throwing rocks, making irritating noises, ripping up a newspaper, and throwing little pieces of paper all over the floor. We didn't accomplish anything. Dr. Harris believed Adam was testing us to see how much he could get away with. No kidding. Dr. Harris is going to meet with Adam alone for the foreseeable future.

* * * *

Mike: Can you explain the difference between an evaluator and a therapist and why Dr. Stone couldn't seem to remember that difference?

Dr. Davies: I can explain the difference between an evaluator and a therapist, but I have no idea why the evaluator in your case took the approach he did. A therapist can be an evaluator, but should not provide therapy on a case where he or she conducted the evaluation.

When the court or a private party hires me, the first thing I do is clarify my role. If I'm hired as an evaluator, my role is to objectively and without bias provide my professional opinion and recommendations. During an evaluation I ask questions and gather information – that's all. If I'm hired as a therapist I also ask questions and gather information; and then I establish treatment goals and provide therapy to help the patient get through a difficult emotional situation.

A psychologist or counselor should avoid dual roles. If the professional is hired as an evaluator, he or she should provide the evaluation quickly and close the case. Dual roles are a violation of my profession's ethical guidelines.

Mike: During an evaluation do you ever reach the point where you figure everything out and then want to switch hats so you can help the patient?

Dr. Davies: I often reach the point where I get a good sense of a situation and mentally map out a course of treatment. But when I'm the evaluator, I don't take on the counselor role until the evaluation is complete and everyone agrees that my role as the counselor is beginning. During an evaluation I might tell the person what I think he or she needs, but if my recommendation includes therapy I won't provide therapy at that point.

Mike: I think Dr. Stone ignored the fact that he was hired as the evaluator and then decided on his own to be the counselor. He compounded the mistake by failing to recognize that Beth wouldn't cooperate.

Dr. Davies: Again, I can't climb inside Dr. Stone's head and tell you why he took the approach he did. However I can tell you that in typical family therapy all the players share the same goal – they want to resolve a problem and heal the family.

In parental alienation cases the players do not share the same goal. The alienating parent has his or her own agenda. A convincing alienating parent may initially pull the wool over the eyes of a competent counselor or therapist. But a good clinician will discover inconsistencies or holes in the alienating parent's story within one or two sessions. When the parent realizes the clinician is no longer passively listening but is instead punching holes in his or her story, the parent banishes the clinician to the enemy camp and stops cooperating. At that point the therapist must take a different approach. Traditional family therapy won't work.

Mike: I couldn't believe how Dr. Stone got so much wrong during his testimony. Let's start with his characterization of my situation as "moderate parental alienation." If my case were a moderate case I would hate to see what a severe case looks like.

Dr. Davies: I'd be interested in knowing what scale he measured your case against. If yours were a moderate case, it would have to be at the very top of the moderate range.

Be that as it may, anyone who the court establishes as an "expert witness" needs to be accurate. There is no excuse for presenting factual information incorrectly.

When I testify as an expert witness, I'm forced to back up my statements with case notes. These notes chart my progress with the patient or family by session. I've sat on the witness stand and gone through notes to substantiate who said something and when he or she said it. In some cases I've gone through a year's worth of progress reports to substantiate a single comment. The court usually accepts my notes as justification for the factual statements I make.

Mike: I also couldn't believe that Stone accepted Adam's position at face value and blamed him for his decisions.

Dr. Davies: It sounds like the evaluator did half his job. He recorded the factual information. That's the first part of the job. But the second part of the job involves taking the alleged facts and testing them – seeing if the information is true. I find that if I push for more details with alienated children and alienating parents the so-called factual information crumbles. A good evaluator should be more than a stenographer. He or she must examine the facts and evaluate them within the context of the family dynamics.

Mike: What do you think of my theory – everything Stone said was aimed at supporting his recommendation for shared custody?

Dr. Davies: I believe in many cases the shared custody recommendation is determined at the outset.

Evaluators know that most judges will not deviate from some variation of shared legal and physical custody in their rulings. For a judge to

165

deviate from shared custody, one side must present compelling factual information and evidence that the child is in immediate danger. Then state regulations require the courts to remove the child from the unhealthy environment.

Evaluators know what circumstances must exist before a judge will remove a child from his home. Your case doesn't meet the criteria – Adam isn't in any immediate physical danger. So your algebra analogy is accurate. Dr. Stone presented the facts that would support a shared custody recommendation. And as I understand the facts of your case, I wouldn't have expected Dr. Stone to reach any other conclusion.

10

Game, Set, Match

May 30

TODAY WAS THE LAST DAY of the trial – the dirtiest, most disgusting week of my life. Every day I walked out of the courthouse and headed straight for the shower. I couldn't wait to scrub off the day's slime.

Beth and her attorney accused me of everything but being the second gunman on the grassy knoll the day President Kennedy was shot. According to Beth's testimony I am a lousy father, an abusive and cheating husband, and a foul-tempered professional who got fired from every job I ever held. They even compared me to O.J. Simpson. If the judge believed their O.J. analogy, my entire legal strategy consisted of outspending Beth and acting "smooth" in order to beat the system and influence the judge into a favorable ruling. Of course, we couldn't tell the judge that the only reason we were having a trial was because of Beth's one-sided demands that gave her sole legal and physical custody of both children and cut me out of their lives.

Attorney Slater and I tried taking a higher road during the trial – although it wasn't all that much higher than the road Beth and her attorney traveled. We brought up her affair in Pennsylvania and reminded Beth on the witness stand that she cheated on her first husband when she began a relationship with me before divorcing him. We painted a picture of a woman who physically and emotionally left her marriage years ago. She wouldn't participate in family activities or go to marriage counseling. Beth only wanted to spend money. We also hit the parental alienation angle hard. Beth deliberately destroyed my relationship with Adam. She still tries to destroy my relationship with Jared. Beth defies court orders that give me time with Adam and "free and liberal" access to Jared when he is with her. Everything we said was true, but I still felt sleazy and disgusting saying it.

The judge wore his disdain for the proceedings like a badge of honor and treated both of us like some foul smelling landfill. His total lack of respect for both the attorneys and litigants was in sharp contrast to the respect he demanded from us. The judge demanded we act contrite, apologetic and timid. He quickly and harshly addressed any display of intelligence or conviction with a sanctimonious and condescending, "I'll-show-him/her-who-is-boss scolding" designed more for putting the offending party back in his or her place than getting at the facts of the case.

The sanctimonious and condescending judge did not issue his decision for more than two weeks. When Lisa finally received it, she quickly called me with the "good" news.

The judge recognized Beth's alienating behavior and addressed it in his decision:

> *"The Husband testified, which was confirmed by Dr. Stone, that prior to the divorce action he enjoyed a good relationship with his son Adam in every way. He alleges that the wife alienated the child against him. While the*

*Husband certainly bears some responsibility for the
dilemma, the court believes that the main responsibility
rests with the Wife who, at the very least inadvertently, or
at the worst intentionally, sent the son the wrong messages
about the father. In the process, the child was led to believe
that his mother needs his support and loyalty."*

We got everything we asked for with respect to Jared and
Adam – practically word for word.

- The judge ignored Beth's request for sole legal and
  physical custody of both kids. His honor gave us joint legal
  of Jared and Adam, and shared physical custody of Jared.
  He ordered us to follow the schedule Jared developed the
  week I moved out of the house. Jared's schedule has him
  spending 15 days with each parent every month.

- The judge issued temporary orders with respect to Adam.
  *"With the goal being that the parenting time between Adam
  and the Husband eventually equate to the liberal,
  reasonable and flexible parenting time that the Husband
  has with Jared,"* the judge wrote. He gave me some time
  with Adam every week in addition to weekly therapy
  sessions with Adam's therapist, Dr. Harris.

- Both Beth and I are required to cooperate with Dr. Harris
  and carry out his recommendations.

A victory? Not really. I was able to protect Jared and our
time together, but the judge's decision was a paper victory as far as
my relationship with Adam.

I'd be a lot more excited about the judge's orders if I
thought Beth would take Adam to therapy or if Adam would spend
some time with me. But the orders aren't worth the paper they're
written on. They're worthless as long as Beth knows the judge
won't punish her or Adam for defying them. The judge said he

169

"considered" my contempt motions in his final decision. However since he did not mention the motions or Beth's refusal to obey court orders anywhere in the 36-page judgment, in reality his honor excused Beth's alienating behavior. The judge sent Beth the clear message that while he may not approve of her behavior, he won't do anything to stop it.

After reviewing the judge's decision, my attorney asked me if I'm relieved. I'm not quite sure how I feel. I'm relieved that the trial is over, and I'm officially divorced. I'm also happy that Beth couldn't disrupt my relationship with Jared. But I feel a big hole in my life where Adam used to be. I felt the hole a long time before the divorce was final, and I suspect I'll feel it for a long time to come.

After spending the better part of the last year in family court, my biggest emotion is disbelief. I can't believe our judicial system is so ineffective. I can't believe a judge, attorneys, court-appointed psychologists and counselors can be so incoherent and blasé about decisions that have a lifelong impact on children. People entering the courthouse are supposed to check cameras, tape recorders and umbrellas at the front door. After the last year, I believe that most of the people working in the courthouse also check their common sense at the front door. I'm convinced that very few of the people I met during this process would keep their jobs in a professionally managed legal or business environment. In the professional world, people are required to meet deadlines and act responsibly. They cannot willfully disregard polices and behave negligently without consequences. In a professional environment, people are held accountable for their actions and can't hide behind someone else's comment to absolve themselves of any responsibility for the outcome of their action. Sadly, no one holds the divorce and child custody professionals I encountered to any of these standards. And to add insult to injury, many of these "professionals" don't treat the litigants, and the problems they bring into the courthouse, with any respect, courtesy or dignity.

Am I angry? You bet. I'm angry with Beth for destroying my relationship with Adam. I'm angry with a judge, Dr. Stone and others who had the power to save Adam from Beth's emotional child abuse but did nothing. I'm angry at a judicial system that is antiquated, broken and ill equipped to deal with alienating parents and alienated children. And I'm angry with anyone who works within the system, recognizes its deficiencies, but looks the other way because of laziness or a vested interest in maintaining the status quo.

If I had fathered a child on the night of July 14, 2004 I most likely would be holding that child in my arms today – totally captivated by the new born infant and daydreaming about the wonderful future we would share together. It's ironic that in the same time I could have had a child – I lost one. What makes the loss harder to bear is that my child didn't die. He is still out there – not even 15 minutes away. When I held Adam in my arms 12 years ago, I never imagined we'd share a future where Adam would rather sit home alone than spend time with me. Once upon a time Adam would break into tears if he watched someone cry. Today he takes perverse delight in watching me cry and knowing he caused my tears.

Twelve years ago I had never heard of parental alienation. When I was in college the term "parental alienation" didn't even exist. However my college roommate, and a friend who took many of the same classes I took, had no contact with their fathers. My roommate felt abandoned. My friend from class told me stories of abuse and abandonment at the hands of her father. At the time, I believed both stories without questioning them. How could any parent do that to a child, I asked myself?

More than twenty years later I'm not so sure these two men abandoned their children. Maybe they did. Maybe the one guy was abusive. I don't know. I do know my friends still believe their fathers abandoned them – just like Adam believes I abandoned him. But maybe these guys just wanted out of bad marriages and their spouses, for whatever reason, pulled the children into the middle of the divorce. Maybe these spouses didn't allow the other parents to build lives with their children that didn't include them?

I don't know whether parental alienation applied to my friends and their fathers. However I do know that alienating behavior has been around for a long time. And I know that the alienating behavior that is part of most divorce and child custody cases today hurts children. I also know that when alienating behavior reaches a certain level, a child is being emotionally abused; and other people shouldn't sit on the sidelines and pretend it isn't happening.

* * * *

Mike: What do you think of the judge's decision?

Dr. Davies: I have a lot of respect for judges who listen to testimony day after day. I really believe they try and reach the best decisions they can.

In your case you wanted the evaluator to stand up and say, "Hey, the child had a great relationship with his father before the divorce action. The mother is causing the child's emotional problems and preventing him from having a normal relationship with his father." Then you wanted the judge to say, "I'll impose consequences on the mother for her behavior so she'll stop it. I'll order the child into therapy, he'll rebuild his relationship with his father, and everyone will live happily ever after." That didn't happen. Both the mental health and judicial systems let you down. And these systems disappoint people like you every day.

I believe judges look at a situation like yours as a domestic dispute between two angry, bitter people who, given enough time, will eventually calm down and work things out. Unless the judge sees obvious signs of physical or sexual abuse, he or she won't take drastic action.

Mike: How about emotional abuse?

Dr. Davies: Generally speaking, judges don't recognize emotional abuse as a valid reason for drastic action. Emotional abuse is difficult to identify. Even more difficult is drawing a cause and effect relationship from emotional abuse to a child's inappropriate behavior.

Mike: How do you define and identify emotional abuse?

Dr. Davies: Emotional child abuse occurs when an adult mistreats a child through words and/or actions and impairs the child's psychological growth and development. Examples of emotional child abuse include putting too many demands on a child, withholding love and affection, excessively discouraging normal behavior like laughing, touching and inquisitiveness, and berating a child for displaying high self-esteem.

Emotional abuse is tough to identify. Unlike physical abuse that leaves bruises on the outside, emotional abuse bruises the child on the inside. Most of the time, a skilled clinician can uncover emotional abuse by watching the child's behavior. An emotionally abused child is often extremely loyal to the abusive parent. The child also displays behavior that is either too mature or too immature for his age. In some case an emotionally abused child will cling excessively to the abusive parent and constantly seek the parent's affection and attention. The child can also be very aggressive, uncooperative and anti-social. He may lack self-confidence, suffer from unusual fears for his age group and have a hard time bonding emotionally with other people.

Since a lot of these behaviors are also found in emotionally healthy children, the key to identifying emotional abuse is determining a change in the child's behavior. If a child never or minimally displayed these characteristics but then began exhibiting these traits, the change in behavior would be a strong indication of emotional abuse.

Mike: If judges don't recognize emotional abuse how can they recognize parental alienation?

Dr. Davies: Judges are just beginning to recognize parental alienation. Parental alienation is a relatively new term. I believe it is a syndrome – a cluster of symptoms as opposed to a diagnostic category like schizophrenia or major depressive disorder. Within the mental health community many psychologists don't recognize parental alienation as a syndrome because it isn't in our DSM – the Diagnostic Statistical Manual we use. If psychologists don't recognize alienation because it isn't included in the DSM, judges certainly won't give it a great deal of consideration before reaching their decisions.

Mike: So that's it. It's over.

Dr. Davies: Legally, it's over. You can file appeals and more contempt motions, but I doubt they'll do any good. You already did everything you could do to influence or change the outcome of a situation that was pre-determined. You tried on your own with Adam and failed. You worked within the mental health and judicial systems and those systems let you down. Any therapy order in place at this time isn't worth the paper it's written on. Judges don't put alienating parents in jail or 12-year-old children in juvenile detention for skipping court-ordered therapy sessions. Technically, the outcome was a tie. The judge ruled right down the middle – shared legal and physical custody. In reality, you lost, and so did Adam.

Mike: So what do I do now?

Dr. Davies: Continue sending Adam consistent messages. Send him birthday cards and presents. Phone him. Send him letters and emails. Invite him places. Just understand his response will be the same for a long time. You're looking at a long process. But you must keep chipping away at his reality.

                At some point Adam will begin individuating and separating emotionally from his mother. At that time he'll start asking himself questions. "If Dad doesn't love me, if he abandoned me, why is he still sending me emails and gifts? Why is he still inviting me places?" The answer to that question, "Dad must want to be in my life," will contradict Adam's long-held beliefs. You can't get Adam to that point. He has to get there himself. But when he does reach that point he'll be ready to work through his anger towards you.

In the meantime, you need to move on emotionally. Stop concentrating on Adam and the relationship you once shared. Concentrate on things you can control. If you continue dwelling on the past, you run the risk of staying angry, becoming anxious and depressed. Your poor emotional health will eventually lead to poor physical health.

Accept the fact that there will be a cloud hanging over you for a number of years. Adam isn't dead. You won't ever feel closure until this situation is resolved. There will be times in the future – holidays, graduations, maybe a chance meeting in a shopping mall – that will bring all your emotions right to the surface. When those events occur you'll have to deal with the pain and heartache all over again. In the meantime, focus on your other child. Focus on your career. Focus on your other relationships and the quality of your life. Find an appropriate outlet for your anger and energy.

11

Why They Do the Things They Do

JUST WHAT IS AN APPROPRIATE outlet for a parent who loses a child to parental alienation, and is, as Dr. Davies described, someone with lots of anger and energy?

The answer came as I described to friends and family members how Beth pulled Adam into the middle of our divorce and made him choose between Mom and Dad. Most everyone asked the same three questions. The first question was, "How can she do that to her child?" The popular follow-up question was always, "Doesn't she realize how she's hurting him?" The third question skipped over the analysis and went straight to the questioner's ideal solution to my problem. "Why can't (fill in the blank -- your attorney, the judge, the psychologist, the police) do anything to help Adam?

I responded to the first two questions with explanations about poor object relations, fear of abandonment and unhealthy bonds between a parent and child. But those explanations didn't address the mental health and legal systems' roles in the parental alienation process.

Beth isn't the first parent to alienate a child from the child's other parent. Nor is Adam the first child to willingly contribute to the alienation campaign. Mental health professionals are finally recognizing that this phenomenon isn't just the normal rancor associated with divorce and child custody cases. Rather, this type of behavior is what psychiatrist Dr. Richard Gardner first identified in the 1980s as Parental Alienation Syndrome (PAS).

I first learned about parental alienation from Gardner's book, *The Parental Alienation Syndrome*. I used to quote chapter and verse from his book to the professionals involved in my case. But Gardner is not without his critics; and his work is often a magnet for controversy.

Gardner's book was self-published, and his detractors claim that his theories are not backed up by research and evidence. Gardner may also have been guilty of a little too much self-promotion; as well as a healthy interest in profiting from his work. Neither trait endeared him to his peers.

Another factor that influences perceptions of Gardner's work is that it is difficult to separate parental alienation from the financial implications of most divorce and child custody cases. Parental alienation often affects custody orders. Custody orders determine child support payments. Individuals and special interest groups have a hard time viewing parental alienation objectively when dollar signs block their view. Someone who believes parental alienation is all about saving one parent money at the expense of the other parent is not typically a fan of the theory or its creator.

I don't believe in throwing the baby out with the bath water, especially since reading *The Parental Alienation Syndrome* was like reading a first-hand account of my experience with Beth and Adam. In addition, I've read other parental alienation articles and talked to many mental health professionals who have experience dealing with this very destructive family dynamic. Dr. Katherine Andre, Dr. Mike Bone, Dr. Douglas Darnell, Dr. Robert Evans, Dr. Jayne A. Major, Dr. Deidre Rand, Dr. Randy Rand, Dr. Reena Sommer and Dr. Richard Warshak are just a few of the professionals who are amazingly consistent in their descriptions parental alienation. If I didn't know better, I would have said they all had front row seats for the drama that had been my life.

In *The Parental Alienation Syndrome*, Gardner says parental alienation is characterized by *both the programming or brainwashing of a child by one parent to denigrate the other parent and the child's own contributions to support the alienating parent's campaign against the previously loved parent.* Adam's contribution to Beth's campaign is the part I had a hard time explaining to my well-meaning friends and family members. No one understood how my previously empathetic, truthful, loving son could become so cruel, dishonest and heartless – including me.

As an alienated parent, I found that intellectually understanding parental alienation provided an emotional anchor. And while understanding alienation doesn't take away the pain of Adam's cruel and insensitive behavior, it does dull the sensation a little bit. Professionals experienced in dealing with parental alienation provide some comfort with their books and articles explaining why these parents and children do the things they do.

In an article entitled *Parents Who Have Successfully Fought Parental Alienation Syndrome* Dr. Jayne A. Major wrote:

I believe that PAS parents have become stuck in the first stage of child development, where survival skills are learned. To them, having total control over their child is a life and death matter. Because they don't understand how to please other people, any effort to do so always has strings attached. They don't give; they only know how to take. They don't play by the rules and are not likely to obey a court order.

Descriptions that are commonly used to describe severe cases of PAS are that the alienating parent is unable to "individuate" (a psychological term used when the person is unable to see the child as a separate human being from him or herself). They are often described as being overly involved with the child or enmeshed.

The parent may be diagnosed as narcissistic (self-centered), he or she presumes that they have a special entitlement to whatever they want. There are rules in life, but only for other people.

Also, he or she may be called a sociopath, which means a person who has no moral conscience. These people are unable to have empathy or compassion for others. They are unable to see a situation from another person's point of view, especially their children's points of view. They don't distinguish between telling the truth and lying in the way that others do.

In spite of admonitions from judges and mental health professionals to stop alienating, they can't. The prognosis for severely alienating parents is poor. It is unlikely that they will ever "get it." It is also unlikely that they will ever stop trying to perpetuate the alienation. It is a gut wrenching survival issue for them.

In his article entitled, *Three Types of Parental Alienators*, Dr. Douglas Darnell describes what he calls "The Obsessed Alienator."

The obsessed alienator is a parent, or sometimes a grandparent, with a cause: to align the children to his or her side and together, with the children, campaign to destroy their relationship with the targeted parent. For the campaign to work, the obsessed alienator enmeshes the children's personalities and beliefs into their own. This is a process that takes time but one that the children, especially the young, are completely helpless to see and combat. It usually begins well before the divorce is final. The obsessed parent is angry, bitter or feels betrayed by the other parent. The initial reasons for the bitterness may actually be justified. They could have been verbally or physically abused, raped, betrayed by an intense affair, or financially cheated. The problem occurs when the feelings won't heal but instead become more intense because of being forced to continue the relationship with a person they despise because of their common parenthood. Just having to see or talk to the other parent is a reminder of the past and triggers the hate. They are trapped with nowhere to go and heal.

The characteristics of obsessed alienators are:

- *They are obsessed with destroying the children's relationship with the targeted parent.*

- *They have succeeded in enmeshing the children's personalities and beliefs about the other parent with their own.*

- *The children will parrot the obsessed alienator rather than express their own feelings from personal experience with the other parent.*

- *The targeted parent and often the children cannot tell you the reasons for their feelings.*

- *Their beliefs sometimes become delusional and irrational. No one, especially the court, can convince obsessed alienators that they are wrong. Anyone who tries is the enemy.*

- *They will often seek support from family members, quasi-political groups or friends that will share in their beliefs that they are victimized by the other parent and the system. The battle becomes "us against them." The obsessed alienator's supporters are often seen at the court hearings even though they haven't been subpoenaed.*

- *They have an unquenchable anger because they believe that the targeted parent has victimized them and whatever they do to protect the children is justified.*

- *They have a desire for the court to punish the other parent with court orders that would interfere or block the targeted parent from seeing the children. This confirms in the obsessed alienator's mind that he or she was right all the time.*

- *The court's authority does not intimidate them.*

- *The obsessed alienator believes in the higher cause, protecting the children at all cost.*

- *The obsessed alienator will probably not want to read this article because the content just makes them angrier.*

Gardner's theory on why alienating parents and children do the things they do is based on psychiatric conditions that may have been present in an alienating parent since childhood. His premise is fairly simple: Many alienating parents walk around suffering from three types of psychopathology generally associated with severe parental alienation – hysteria, paranoia or psychopathy. To the rest of the world these people exhibit very few outward indications that something not quite right lurks just beneath the surface. Like everyone else, they have successes and failures at work. They have the normal ups and downs raising their families. To the rest of the world these people may even appear healthier and happier than most. Doesn't the grass usually look greener on the other side of the fence?

What puts these people on the road to alienating behavior, according to Gardner, is stress. Stress over the divorce. Stress over an unknown future. Stress due to a change in their financial situation. Stress over feeling a loss of control. Stress of old abandonment issues resurfacing. Gardner indicated these disorders are reactive – environmental stressors kick them into high gear. Parents suffering from hysteria, paranoia or psychopathy, or any combination of the three, only exhibit mild symptoms until they get stressed out over issues associated with the divorce. People probably couldn't detect mild symptoms of these disorders under normal circumstances. In stressful situations, those same disorders become examples of parental alienation that become as plain as the nose on the alienating parent's face.

Hysteria

The *2001 Merriam-Webster Dictionary* defines hysteria as a:

1. Psychoneurosis marked by emotional excitability and disturbances of the psychic, sensory, vasomotor, and visceral functions.

2. Behavior exhibiting overwhelming or unmanageable fear or emotional excess.

Most people get upset. But even by a standard reference definition hysterical people would seem much more likely to get upset more often and to a much greater degree than average people.

Gardner recognizes that parents who induce parental alienation in their children are often quite emotional – especially when it comes to describing the indignities the targeted parent allegedly heaped on the child. Further, alienating parents typically overreact in situations that others would not consider a cause for concern. Alienating parents often see danger in situations where danger does not exist.

Gardner also points out that while many people with psychiatric symptoms often suffer in silence, hysterical people attract significant attention. The hysterical alienating parent quickly learns that this attention is an excellent source of sympathy, support and even validation.

Finally, according to Gardner, hysteria allows alienating parents to release anger in a way that they believe is socially acceptable. They can focus their anger on the person that they believe is dangerous. The hysterical alienating parent essentially tells the world, "Look how much grief this person has caused me. Look how afraid this person makes me. Look how dangerous this person is."

Paranoia

Paranoia is a form of delusion. Delusions are false ideas that have no basis in reality. While there are many different kinds of delusions, paranoia is a specific kind of delusion in which the individual believes others are persecuting him or her when there is no justification for such a belief.

According to Gardner, paranoia includes six characteristics central to the paranoid alienating parent's core belief system:

- **Projection.** Remember the old Bible verse, "Do unto others as you would have them do unto you?" Paranoid people, "Project onto others what they do unto others but can't admit they do." The paranoids can't accept that their negative thoughts and feelings are unacceptable. By projecting these thoughts and feelings onto others, the paranoids pronounce themselves clean and acceptable.

  For example, an alienating parent accuses the other parent of denigrating him or her in front of their child. The targeted parent's name-calling and disrespectful attitude towards him or her, the parent says, is why the child wants nothing to do with the targeted parent. When asked by therapists and court-ordered counselors if he or she might have ever, even in a moment of anger or frustration, said anything negative about the other parent in front of the child, the alienating parent typically replies, "Never. I would never talk like that in front of the kids."

- **Oversimplification.** Paranoids oversimplify everything. They don't recognize that problems are often complex – the result of multiple factors. Paranoids also believe solving problems are simple – yet only they are capable of coming up with the easy solutions. The alienating parent believes the previously loved parent is solely responsible for his or her estranged relationship with the child. Further, the alienating parent may tell those same court-ordered counselors that the child would be fine and "come around" if everyone just left him or her alone. Therapy isn't necessary. Neither is court-ordered time with the other parent. The alienating parent will go to great lengths to prevent the child from hearing something that would contradict the very simple, "good guy vs. bad guy" scenario at the foundation of his or her successful alienation campaign. The parent could also ignore any professional recommendation that doesn't fit with his or her oversimplified alienation campaign. To consider such a recommendation would force the parent to admit that his or her position may not be correct and in the child's best interest.

- **Reality.** Paranoia is a form of delusion based on internal forces rather than external realities. Paranoids will resist anyone's attempt to bring them face-to-face with reality because reality conflicts with the internal forces creating the delusion. Anyone who tries forcing a paranoid to accept reality better prepare for a long, frustrating afternoon. First the paranoid person will try avoiding the conversation. If the paranoid is unsuccessful avoiding the conversation, he or she will come up with enough illogical reasons for the position that the person who initiated the conversation will walk away baffled and muttering, "I wouldn't believe what I just heard if I hadn't heard it with my own two ears."

An alienating parent is totally unaffected by judges, attorneys, psychologists, family members or friends who confront the parent with a reality different from what he or she believes is true. Despite evidence that the formerly loved parent is not the affront to parenting and humanity that the alienator believes him or her to be, the alienator maintains his or her position. The alienating parent knows "what that person is really like." If a judge or psychologist comes to a conclusion other than the alienating parent's conclusion, the parent believes the professional was, "taken in" by the targeted parent or is unfairly siding with the targeted parent – thus automatically disqualifying the professional from ever having an objective opinion worthy of consideration. Naturally, if a psychologist and judge support the alienating position, the alienating parent commends them for their brilliance, experience and courage.

- **Low Self-Esteem.** Paranoids have low self-esteem and are insecure. Their insecurity is one reason they "project onto others." Most people are secure enough to have the occasional socially unacceptable thought and understand that these thoughts are okay as long as they don't act on them. But paranoids aren't secure enough to realize these thoughts are normal. Paranoids believe these thoughts are a character flaw or deficiency. So they deny their thoughts by projecting them onto others.

People with low self-esteem also find it difficult to admit that they are wrong – ever. Remember the old platitude, "It takes a big man to admit he is wrong?" The word "big" didn't refer to the person's overall size; but rather, the size of the individual's ego. A person with a healthy ego has no trouble admitting he or she is wrong. Paranoids can't admit they're wrong – even in the face of

186

facts, logic and experts – because admitting they're wrong is too painful. They don't have the ego to admit they could be wrong but still be a good person. Another reason judges, attorneys, psychologists, family members and friends can't order or convince an alienating parent to stop alienating is because if he or she stopped alienating, the parent would have to admit his or her original position was wrong. The parent can't do that.

- **The Spread.** The paranoids' delusions may start with a single target, but paranoid people quickly widen their delusional fields to include everyone associated with their situations. Paranoids live in a black and white world. There is no room for gray in the delusional thought process. They believe "you're either with me or against me." Alienating parents start by spreading their distortions and delusions to their children. Then they move on to friends, co-workers and family members. Finally, they attempt to convince attorneys, psychologists, and judges of the righteousness of their position. For the alienating parent, deciding who is trustworthy is simple. Anyone who supports the alienation campaign is a white-hat-wearing good guy. Anyone who suggests his or her position is not just and correct is a black-hat-wearing bad guy. In the alienating parent's world, the bad guys quickly take their rightful place alongside the now-despised targeted parent – outside the inner circle and cut off from the child. These bad guys may include previously loved and respected aunts, uncles, grandparents and close family friends. The alienating parent will never consider an opinion or idea from someone outside the circle. Their motives are suspect. They're aligned with the despised parent and "up to no good." Conversely, anyone inside the circle is trustworthy and is immediately bestowed advanced degrees in psychology and the law. These people become experts for one simple reason – the alienating parent shares their expert opinions. These "good guys," like the alienating parent, profess to have the child's best interests at heart. However, in their zeal to be a good friend, empathetic co-worker or supportive family member they forget the first rule of human relationships – there are two sides to every story.

- **Cruelty.** Paranoids can be extremely cruel. They justify their cruelty with a "get them before they get you" mentality that allows them to strike out at anyone they believe is persecuting them. Paranoids may even believe they're performing a public service of sorts by attacking a menace to society. The alienating parent has no conscience when it comes to the cruel indignities he or she piles on the previously loved parent. He or she has no empathy for the pain over the loss of the parent-child relationship. Quite the contrary. The alienating parent enjoys his or her suffering. After all, according to the alienating parent, the now-hated parent got what he or she deserved. The parent doesn't even acknowledge that his or her actions hurt the child – the very person the parent says he or she is trying to protect. For alienating parents, the end justifies the means – no matter what the cost.

Psychopathy

According to Gardner, psychopathy generally refers to a personality disorder that endures. However Gardner emphasizes that the psychopathic characteristics present in parental alienation may not have been present in the alienating parent's makeup prior to the divorce or the child-custody battle. Some alienating parents may have had psychopathic tendencies prior to the litigation. But other alienating parents didn't become psychopathic until the onset of their legal battles. Here are the characteristics of psychopathic behavior and how they look within the context of parental alienation:

- **Nonconformity to the Social Order.** Quite simply, psychopaths don't follow the rules. They arrogantly believe rules do not apply to them. An alienating parent believes the judge's orders are for everyone else. The parent may not stand up in court and refuse to obey the order, but at the end of the day you can count on the fact that the order was disobeyed. Active resistance or passive resistance is still resistance.

- **Reflex Commitment to the Pleasure Principle.** Psychopaths want what they want when they want it. Much like the child who eats too much candy without considering the stomachache just around the corner; psychopaths live for the moment without considering the long-term consequences of their acts. An alienating parent striking out at the previously loved parent gets immediate gratification every time the child refuses to see or talk to the other parent. The alienating parent immensely enjoys seeing the other person in pain. However I've often wondered if alienating parents believe they can reverse the alienation one day down the road in order to satisfy some other need they may have at that particular moment. But much like the child who doesn't see the stomachache coming, alienating parents don't realize that once they let the genie out of the bottle, the genie doesn't go back.

- **Absence of Shame and/or Guilt.** Psychopaths never feel shame or guilt – those uncomfortable feelings that go hand-in-hand with getting caught doing something that you know others consider unacceptable. They don't feel shame – the emotion most people feel when they get exposed. Nor do they feel guilt – the internally driven feeling of low self-worth that most people instinctively feel when they do something wrong. The alienating parent rarely feels shame or guilt over the cruel indignities he or she heaps on the other parent. This parent sees nothing wrong with asking the previously loved parent to buy presents for the child knowing full well that the child won't even acknowledge receiving the gifts. The alienating parent also doesn't feel shame or guilt over excluding the other parent from school conferences, birthday parties, graduation ceremonies, ball games, medical consultations and other activities. Of course, he or she has no conscience about asking the parent to pay for these activities – the alienating parent just doesn't see any reason why the other parent should expect to be invited.

- **Absence of Empathy and/or Sympathy.** Empathy is the ability to see the world through someone else's eyes. Sympathy is the ability to feel what someone else feels. Psychopaths don't possess either ability. They can't see a situation from someone else's perspective or identify with their pain. These missing emotions are an asset to an alienating parent. Without any understanding of the pain they're causing the formerly loved Mom or Dad, the alienating parent is emotionally free to inflict bigger, more vicious and sadistic indignities on the target.

- **Impulsivity.** Psychopaths are very impulsive. They live in the present and don't consider the future. Their impulsiveness is designed for immediate and maximum gratification. An alienating parent can be very impulsive – especially when the estranged parent tries breaking through the impenetrable wall the alienating parent has built around child. Slamming down the phone, unilaterally canceling parenting time and calling the police are just some of an alienating parent's impulsive responses to dealing with the formerly loved parent.

- **Impaired Ability to Form Stable Human Relationships.** Psychopaths typically suffer from damaged childhood object relations. They are incapable of having long-term healthy adult relationships because they never learned about healthy relationships as a child. As adults they display a general inability to maintain long-term stable relationships with friends, family members and spouses. In the case of an alienating parent, this deficiency contributes to the breakdown of the marriage. The alienating parent generally has a poor sense of self and poor boundaries. These traits contribute to his or her inability to trust, discuss opposing viewpoints, compromise and successfully negotiate the solutions to normal differences of opinions. Since the alienating parent often defines himself or herself in terms of someone else, his or her deficiency also contributes to the need to form an emotionally unhealthy co-dependent relationship with the child. This deficiency prevents the alienating parent from ever developing a healthy post-divorce detente with the ex-spouse. The life-long inability to form stable human relationships and the need to see the ex-spouse as the enemy is what allows the alienating parent to destroy the child's healthy bond with the targeted parent.

- **Deceit.** Don't ever play poker with a psychopath. Psychopaths are great liars. They'll look you right in the eye, keep a straight face, profess their honesty, and then proceed to recite one lie after another. Psychopaths are such accomplished liars they would probably pass a polygraph test, because they believe what they say. An alienating parent lies constantly to see and define him or herself as good and righteous. The parent lies to the alienated child in order to strengthen his or her position and justify his or her cause. The parent lies to friends and family members in order to enlist their support in the alienation campaign. The parent lies to psychologists, teachers, counselors, attorneys and judges in order to maintain the alienated child's status quo. Most of all, the alienating parent lies to himself or herself – convinced that the negative and destructive actions are motivated by a great love for the child and the need to protect the child from the previously loved and respected other parent.

- **Manipulation.** Deceit and manipulation are the psychopath's one-two punch. A psychopath leads with a lie and follows with a convincing, plausible con job. Remember Robert Redford and Paul Newman in *The Sting*? Their characters were so smooth, attractive and articulate that audiences had no problem rooting for them. The alienating parent also cons people into rooting for him or her. The parent deliberately twists facts, misinterpret positive overtures from the other parent and misrepresent the intentions of psychologists and helping professionals. While judges and psychologists don't always fall for the con, one person always does – the child. The child is too gullible to resist being taken in by someone he has spent his whole life trusting.

- **Anger and Sadism.** Psychopaths can be very cruel. Remember, empathy and sympathy are foreign concepts to psychopaths. Without these constraints psychopaths are free to indulge themselves at the expense of other people. An alienating parent primarily indulges himself or herself at the expense of one other person – the previously loved spouse and parent. His or her cruelty and sadistic behavior towards the parent knows no boundaries or limits. The alienated child participates in the campaign of denigration as well. The child enjoys seeing his or her behavior strike a chord. To the child, a tear running down the alienated parent's face is victory.

- **Irresponsibility.** You can't ever count on a psychopath to say the same thing twice. They say what sounds plausible to fill an immediate need without giving any thought to how their comments compare to what they said in the past or what they may have to say in the future. The alienating parent's overall goals are to "protect" the child from the previously loved parent and to shield himself or herself from criticism and negative feedback. If need be, he or she will change the story in the blink of an eye to achieve his or her goals. If someone dares to point out the inconsistency, the alienating parent immediately questions that person's credibility and motives. The alienating parent will ultimately banish anyone who challenges him or her too often to a place outside the trusted circle and far away from the child – with little or no concern for the long-term effects on the child's emotional well-being.

- **Disloyalty and Betrayal.** Psychopaths are loyal to one, and only one, person – themselves. Their life experiences have taught them that relationships are disposable. They keep everyone at arm's length to avoid getting hurt. Sure, they may profess loyalty to others; but their statements are rarely backed up with actions and are designed primarily to make themselves feel good about themselves. An alienating parent who destroys an otherwise healthy bond between a parent and child rationalizes the actions as loyalty to the child. In the parent's mind the child is the one person who won't leave or betray his or her trust. However these actions are anything but loyalty. Rather, the alienating parent's actions are the ultimate betrayal. The alienating parent betrays the child's trust by lying to and manipulating him in order to fulfill his or her own emotional needs. In the process, the parent destroys the child's ability to grow and develop independently.

- **Punishment is No Deterrent.** It would be misleading to represent that punishment does not deter psychopaths, so therefore punishment does not deter the alienating parent. As Gardner observed, many alienating parents do not demonstrate psychopathic tendencies prior to the divorce or the child-custody battle. Therefore, an alienating parent's behavior shouldn't be lumped together with clinically diagnosed psychopathic behaviors. Psychopathic behavior is anti-social and often illegal despite society's very real threat of jail time or other severe consequences. An alienating parent *might* change his or her behavior if he or she believed punishment was imminent and severe. Unfortunately, most courts teach the alienating parent that punishment is non-existent. Judges routinely grant multiple delays and second, third, fourth and fifth chances in most civil courtrooms. They rarely use the three deterrents – loss of custody, money and jail time – at their disposal when dealing with an alienating parent. Unlike physical and sexual child abuse cases – where evidence of the abuse is legally outlined and too apparent to ignore – alienation and emotional child abuse cases do not evoke the same reaction from the courts. Most judges consider parental alienation nothing more than bad parenting; and bad parenting is not a crime. Judges often threaten the alienating parent who fails to obey court orders with jail time, loss of financial support or even loss of the child; but their threats are usually nothing more than hot air. Judges simply don't incarcerate a mother or father who fails to bring the child to court-ordered counseling sessions. The parent quickly learns that judges are unwilling to back up their threats with actions, so his or her alienation campaign continues.

- **The End Justifies the Means.** No guilt, no sympathy, no empathy, no problem. Psychopaths' inability to feel guilt, sympathy and empathy make it easier for them to do whatever it takes to reach their goal. Remember, the alienating parent believes his or her goal is the noblest act – protecting the child from the previously loved but now despised other parent. The parent will do anything to keep the child safe. There is no greater cause. An absence of guilt, sympathy and empathy for the targeted parent helps bury the formerly loved spouse under a mountain of humiliation, indignities, false accusations and legal motions, all designed to keep him or her from having a healthy relationship with the child. The alienating parent also has no remorse about subjecting the child to the emotional conflict that comes with programming the child to contribute to the alienation campaign. After all, if the parent was wrong would the child be devoted to him or her and angry with the other parent? Of course not. The alienating parent knows best, and the end justifies the means.

- **Pride in Antisocial Behavior.** Psychopaths are typically very proud of their behavior. So is the alienating parent. The alienating parent's only problem is he or she can't boast of the successful alienation campaign to the world. Sure, the alienating parent will share his or her success with trusted friends and family members, but even then he or she must camouflage his or her true feelings. To allies the alienating parent will display pride in protecting the child from the horrible person formerly known as Mom or Dad. But to judges, psychologists, counselors and anyone else he or she must discuss the situation with; the alienating parent will express deep regret and empathy for the now despised other parent. "I want my child to have a relationship with his other parent," he or she will say earnestly. Of course, the parent is consciously lying. A relationship between the child and the other parent is the last thing an alienating parent wants. However lying to the professionals is a means to an end. The parent understands that hiding his or her pride from people who aren't trustworthy is a small price to pay for achieving the goal. The only time alienating parents will truly allow themselves to take pride in their actions is when they are alone.

- **Rationalization.** Psychopaths rationalize their behavior. Rationalization is the only way psychopaths can effectively deceive themselves into believing that their anti-social behavior is somehow acceptable. The alienating parent often rationalizes his or her behavior for similar reasons. "I have to fight fire with fire. All's fair in love and war. I'll do anything to protect my child." Rationalizing that his or her negative and destructive acts are the only effective way to protect the child makes the actions, at least in his or her own mind, acceptable and justified.

An alienated parent can't read these explanations without thinking about his or her own situation and looking for an answer to the question, "How could the other parent do this to a child?" Does the parent suffer from hysteria, paranoia and a personality disorder? Did these factors contribute to the alienating behavior?

A few paragraphs in a book won't give me, or anyone else, a definitive answer. I just keep coming back to Gardner's definition of parental alienation – *both the programming or brainwashing of a child by one parent to denigrate the other parent and the child's own contributions to support the alienating parent's campaign against the previously loved parent.*

* * * *

Dr. Davies: You've been doing some reading.

Mike: You said I should find an appropriate outlet for my anger and energy. Besides, reading up on the subject is validating.

Dr. Davies: It is very important for an alienated parent intellectually and logically to understand parental alienation in order to gain some control over, and emotional distance from, a very personal and painful situation. An alienated parent needs the intellectual context for what is happening in his or her life. This perspective helps the parent avoid emotional reactions. Purely emotional reactions are unhealthy and can lead to bad decisions; not to mention a variety of physical and emotional problems.

Mike: I recognized a lot of psychological concepts in the articles and books from our conversations. Do all parental alienation cases come down to the same basic elements?

Dr. Davies: Yes. I believe some basic sociopathic elements are at work in all alienating parents. These elements may lie dormant for years, but when the divorce, the ultimate adult abandonment, becomes real, the alienating parent becomes symptomatic. The evidence of these elements – the person's inability to trust, compromise or connect with others – is always present. It just takes a trained eye to identify it.

Mike: So parental alienation is never just emotionally healthy people taking out their anger on the previously loved spouse?

Dr. Davies: Is an iceberg ever just the part that sits above the water line? Or does the iceberg go much deeper than what you see on the surface?

In parental alienation, the anger and hate are symptomatic of an alienating parent who needs to create psychological and emotional distance from old, painful, unresolved issues. Those issues remain dormant as long as the alienating parent doesn't feel betrayed or abandoned. But when the spouse leaves, the alienating parent is forced to confront issues he or she buried long ago. The alienating parent comes face-to-face with his or her own vulnerability over issues that are very familiar and painful. These issues are so significant that the alienating parent needs the child to help confront these issues. The child helps the alienating parent change his or her focus. The parent is now protecting the child. This

197

new focus allows the parent's painful and unwanted emotions to subside. The hate and anger the parent experiences are reactions to his or her painful emotions, but the alienating parent projects these feelings at the other parent in order to justify his or her response as normal behavior. After all, the formerly loved spouse is now trying to hurt the parent and child. Once the child helps the alienating parent put some distance between the parent and his or her old issues, the anger and hate subside to a spot just below the surface.

Mike: Do the rest of us have buried unresolved issues that must stay buried so we can function?

Dr. Davies: Clinically speaking, we all have a variety of neurosis, idiosyncrasies and quirks that make us who we are. Most of the time people ignore or accept our individual differences if they are within what society considers "normal limits."

The difference, as Gardner pointed out, is how we deal with stress. We all have limits on our ability to incorporate and synthesize new information. We translate this new information into coping skills so we can adapt and deal with normal day-to-day events. When we're forced to deal with unresolved issues on top of our everyday events, our coping skills become strained and we become "stressed out." This is when our defenses break down.

Someone who is a little obsessive compulsive will become very obsessive compulsive under stress. A person prone to hysterical behavior will become more hysterical when his or her

defenses break down. Paranoids become more
paranoid.

Mike: How much of the increased behavior is
really due to stress and broken down defenses and
how much of it is positive reinforcement? If
someone acts hysterically and gets the desired
response, it just stands to reason that acting more
hysterical will result in an even more desirable
response.

Dr. Davies: The hysterical alienating parent follows a
typical pattern or stimulus, response and behavioral
reinforcement. In behavioral psychology terms, if a
behavior is followed by a positive result, the chance
of that behavior recurring or increasing is greater.
Does this mean the hysterical alienating parent is
acting, or faking the behavior, to receive a better
response? I don't believe so.

    If the parent was intelligent and
manipulative before the hysterical outbursts than it
stands to reason that he or she will be intelligent and
manipulative during the outbursts. The parent is
capable of turning up the dial to ensure a better
outcome. However the hysterical alienating parent's
number one priority is to regain control any way he
or she can. All the parent's defenses have broken
down. The parent has minimal coping skills and an
overwhelming desire to flee from a painful
emotional experience. His or her behavior may
appear like acting to an emotionally healthy person
who can't understand what all the fuss is about, but
the emotions causing the outburst are very real to
the hysterical alienating parent.

| Mike: | How do psychologists treat a person who is prone to hysteria? |

Dr. Davies: Psychologists who treat hysterics want to help them regain some sense of control over their life via therapy or medication.

True hysterics typically need medication to help reduce their symptoms. Usually these people are too symptomatic to treat without medication. However, once a hysteric's symptoms are reduced, a combination of relaxation exercises and other cognitive behavioral techniques can be quite effective in helping the individual regain a sense of control.

Mike: What do you tell an alienated parent who is on the receiving end of the hysterical behavior?

Dr. Davies: The best advice I can give an alienated parent is to stop participating. Let go of the rope. Don't offer resistance. It's tough to stop a runaway train, but the train does eventually stop when it runs out of fuel. A hysterical alienating parent needs a stimulus to fuel his or her behavior. The behavior can't sustain itself on its own. If the alienated parent doesn't provide the fuel, the behavior will eventually die out. Of course, the alienating parent will probably find another source of fuel in order to maintain his or her pattern of behavior and continue in the victim's role; but at least the alienated parent isn't providing it.

Mike: How does paranoid behavior manifest itself in parental alienation? What does it look like?

Dr. Davies: Paranoia and other irrational fears are based on emotional conclusions. Paranoids reinforce their conclusions by avoiding situations that may invoke a negative response. For example, if a paranoid believes someone is tapping his or her telephone conversations in an attempt to gather incriminating evidence, the paranoid won't use the phone – in effect strengthening his or her belief system.

In parental alienation the alienating parent is operating from the faulty premise that the other parent is the enemy, and he or she is out to hurt and destroy my child and me. From this firmly held position, the alienating parent distorts reality to fit his or her perception of the world. The parent creates a tightly knit way of looking at things so anyone who challenges his or her reality is seen as a potential threat or harm to his or her well-being.

A paranoid alienating parent rarely accepts anything at face value. He or she will analyze each situation and look for ulterior motives. If the other parent says he or she is taking the child to the beach for the day, the paranoid alienating parent may believe the other parent's real plan is to kidnap the child.

Mike: Can you counsel and provide therapy to a paranoid alienating parent?

Dr Davies: Working with a paranoid patient is similar to working with a hysterical patient. The psychologist needs to help both patients regain a sense of control in their lives. However the professional's job is more difficult in paranoid cases because the paranoid's belief system is based on emotion and resistant to logic.

To treat paranoia and/or irrational fears, the professional must help the patient break down the pieces into smaller, less fearful elements. Psychologists do this by setting up a list, or hierarchy, of fears for the patient that goes from "least feared" to "most feared."

I always start at the low end of the hierarchy. For example, say a person is afraid of taking an elevator to the 20th floor because of an irrational fear of heights or closed-in spaces. This person will start feeling anxious and a loss of control hours before he or she ever gets on the elevator – sometimes even before leaving the house. I would teach this person relaxation techniques such as breathing exercises and visual imagery so he or she can initially remain calm at home.

Then I'd move up the hierarchy. I would hope to use the same relaxation techniques to get the person to the point where he or she is comfortable driving to the building that contains the elevator. The next step in the hierarchy may be getting the person to enter the building's lobby, followed by getting the person to take the elevator to the fifth floor. The ultimate goal is to for the person to gain enough control to ride the elevator to the 20th floor.

Mike: If working with a paranoid is difficult, what is it like working with a psychopathic alienating parent?

Dr. Davies: Impossible. True psychopaths resist change. As you mentioned, psychopaths have no conscience. They don't connect their behavior to the consequences of their behavior. They can do anything without feeling guilt, shame or humiliation. It is very difficult to counsel someone an hour a week when they spend the rest of the week in an environment based on a faulty belief system.

The best place to treat a psychopath is in a controlled environment. In this environment you can keep showing the psychopath the consequences of his or her behavior. Hopefully the psychopath will eventually internalize the reality that his or her behavior causes a specific reaction or negative consequence.

Mike: What do you tell an alienated parent who is on the receiving end of psychopathic behavior?

Dr. Davies: There's not much you can tell anyone who is the target of psychopathic alienating behavior. Knowledge and intellectually understanding the situation are important. The alienated parent also should set clear boundaries between him or herself and the psychopath. Unfortunately, in parental alienation those boundaries also become boundaries between an alienated parent and the child he or she wants so desperately to reconnect with. There is no easy answer.

12

Three Levels of Parental Alienation

I ALWAYS MARVELED AT THE VERBAL switch that gets thrown in parents' heads shortly after a divorce. Faster than newly divorced parents can say "good riddance," they typically start disassociating themselves from the other parent when talking to the child they conceived together. "You'll be spending next weekend with *your* father" replaces "You'll be spending next weekend with Dad." "*Your* mother is on the phone" takes the place of "Mom is on the phone." A parent who inserts the word "your" before every reference to the other parent is gently saying, "You're still connected to him/her. I'm not." It's as if the child's connection to the previously loved spouse should come with a warning label.

While not in the same league as an all-out assault on a healthy parent/child relationship, this subtle change in language is also a form, albeit a very mild form, of parental alienation.

I wasn't surprised that there are different levels of parental alienation. People typically measure behavior along a continuum.

The best behavior is at one end of the continuum and the worst behavior is at the other end of the continuum. In-between the two end points there are degrees of the behavior that people label for easy-to-understand reference points.

Parental alienation is no different. While professionals use different labels to describe three parental alienation reference points, most professional essentially came to the same conclusion. Parental alienation is like an appliance with three speeds – low, medium and high.

Low a.k.a. Appropriate Parenting

Let's be honest – even a divorced parent-of-the-year candidate will occasionally say something negative to the child about the other parent out of frustration over a disagreement. After all, if the former spouses never disagreed or got frustrated with each other they would still be married. In addition, divorced parents are often accustomed to having frustrations boil over in front of the child from their days of living under the same roof. These parents inevitably fought in front of the child – no matter how careful they were to hide their disagreements. Most houses aren't big enough or sound proof enough to protect the child from *ever* hearing Mom and Dad fight.

These divorced parents are low-level alienators because they said something negative about the other parent to their child, regretted the outburst, worried about the effect it would have on the child, and took steps to explain their inappropriate behavior. In short, low-level alienators are human – and good parents.

The low-level alienator recognizes that the child needs to have a normal, healthy, loving relationship with the other parent. The low-level alienator is generally supportive of the other parent and even facilitates the normal growth and development of that relationship. This parent is able to separate the child's needs from his or her own, and despite the occasional "*Your* mother is on the phone" or "I wish your father would grow up and act like a responsible adult" type comment, puts aside his or her own feelings about the divorce and communicates with his or her former spouse so the child's needs are met.

Basically, low-level alienators display all the qualities of good parents and normal, emotionally healthy adults. A low-level alienator may say something negative out of frustration, but:

- Does not have unresolved dependency or abandonment issues.

- Won't blame the other parent when something is wrong in his or her life.

- Supports the child's emotional development by seeing the child's needs as separate and independent from his or her own.

- Is secure enough in his or her own relationship with the child to encourage the child to have a normal, healthy relationship with the other parent.

- Respects the child's privacy when it comes to the child's life with the other parent.

- Works with the other parent so the child doesn't suffer or get caught in the middle of a situation involving the adults.

- Feels guilty when he or she lets his or her emotions get the best of him or her and says something negative about the other parent in front of the child.

- Apologizes to the child and explains the outburst was not a true reflection of what he or she believes.

Low-level alienators don't damage their child's relationship with the other parent because they recognize the negative behavior and correct themselves before their behavior gets out of control. These parents know they occasionally make mistakes, but have a healthy enough attitude to correct those mistakes. They might not always want to do the right thing, but they usually do the right thing without regret because they know what's right is what's best for their child.

Medium a.k.a. Reactive Parenting

As the word "medium" suggests, medium-level alienators fall somewhere between the two parental alienation extremes.

On the one hand, medium-level alienators mean well. They believe their child should have a normal, healthy relationship with the other parent. But on the other hand, they also believe that normal healthy relationship shouldn't come at their expense. Nor should their child's good relationship with the other parent in any way interfere with their life.

This type of alienating behavior is usually short-lived. Medium-level alienators begin the behavior after some real or perceived slight from the other parent. These alienators have a hard time controlling their emotions and their full-fledged parental alienation assault on the other parent will last as long as their emotional reaction lasts. Their actions are brash, foolhardy, hotheaded and ill considered. When medium level alienators get over their anger, these parents stop the alienating behavior and move on. At this point they once again recognize that their child needs a normal, healthy, loving relationship with the targeted parent. While they may not go out of their way to facilitate the development of the relationship, or even actively encourage it, at least the medium-level alienators aren't actively sabotaging the relationship. That is, until the next time they believe the other parent is doing something that is not in their or their child's best interests. Then the alienating behavior begins all over again.

Medium-level alienators' behavior has a lot to do with impulsive responses and a loss of control to specific events – usually a real or perceived act of aggression from the other parent. All people react differently when they're angry than they react under normal circumstances. Medium-level alienators are no different in that respect. However medium-level alienators' anger is always directed towards the other parent. Their unhealthy solution for dealing with their anger is to use the child as a weapon against the targeted parent.

When medium-level alienators actively disrupt their child's relationship with the other parent, their campaign typically extends to the targeted parent's family and friends. The alienating parents broaden their alienation campaign without any guilt or empathy for the people they are hurting – including the child.

High a.k.a. Obsessed Parenting

High-level alienators are alienators with a mission – destroy the previous healthy and loving relationship between their child and the targeted parent. These alienators are obsessed and relentless. They never get tired, stop scheming or pass up an opportunity to reinforce their destructive messages to the child. They conscript friends, family members, neighbors, co-workers, police officers and social service agencies into their battle against the targeted parent. High-level alienators manipulate attorneys', psychologists and judges in order to turn potential "decision makers" into allies. These alienating parents are walking examples of the paranoid and psychopathic behavior described in the previous chapter. Nothing will satisfy these people short of the total, complete and permanent destruction of the previously loving and healthy relationship between the child and targeted parent. And even then they may not be finished.

Once the alienation is complete and irreversible, unsatisfied high-level alienators may use the child in an attempt to continue exacting revenge on the previously loved spouse. Together parent and child can run up unnecessary bills aimed at leaving the targeted/responsible parent in debt. They can make false physical or sexual abuse allegations aimed at branding the targeted parent an abusive parent or sex offender. They can make false statements to the police in an attempt to get the targeted parent arrested and jailed. High-level alienators looking to make the targeted parent suffer indignity and hardship tap a bottomless source of creativity that only hatred, obsession and vindictiveness can fuel.

Practically speaking, here are just a few examples of high-level alienator behavior:

- Allow the child to talk negatively or disrespectfully about the other parent.

- Set up tempting alternatives that would interfere with the other parent's time with the child.

- Give the child decision-making power about spending time with the targeted parent when no choice exists.

- Act hurt and betrayed if the child shows any positive feelings towards the targeted parent.

- Use the child as a courier, messenger or spy.

- Ask the child to lie to the other parent or betray the parent's trust in the child.

- Share the details of the divorce settlement with the child.

- Go without dinner and then tell the child the other parent didn't give them enough money for everyone to eat dinner.

- Disconnect the phone or take it off the hook so the targeted parent can't get through.

- Let the targeted parent worry needlessly about the child.

- Infringe on the other parent's time with excessive phone calls or scheduled activities.

And here are just a few things a high-level alienator will never do:

- Buy birthday cards and holiday presents for a younger child to give to the other parent.

- Inform the child when the other parent calls or reminds the child to call the other parent when a call is expected.

- Make sure the other parent gets report cards, school picture order forms and invitations to school plays, graduations and recitals.

- Inform the other parent about the child's illnesses and injuries.

- Drive the child back and forth between the households.

- Put pictures of the other parent in the child's room.

- Demonstrate flexibility with the other parent to allow for vacations and unexpected events.

- Allow the child to take personal possessions over to the other parent's home.

- Communicate with the other parent to resolve conflict.

High-level alienators possess a single-minded sense of purpose only found in the most driven individuals. Their need to destroy the previously loved other parent's relationship with the child becomes a crusade. This crusade provides high-level alienators with an unhealthy outlet for their emotions.

211

When high-level alienators are in the throes of an alienation campaign, the child is both a weapon to be used against the alienated parent and a tool to make high-level alienators feel emotionally complete. They rarely stop to consider how their actions affect the child. If they do consider the child, high-level alienators quickly address those thoughts with simple behavior-reinforcing platitudes such as, "I know what's best," "Whatever it takes," and "It's the other parent's fault." High-level alienators are neither aware of nor interested in, the confusion and conflicted emotions raging inside their child. Nor do they concern themselves with the child's future. High-level alienators are only interested in satisfying their own unhealthy internally driven needs. These parents don't take responsibility for their actions. If the alienated child ultimately has problems in school, with relationships, drugs or alcohol, the high-level alienator will quickly identify the targeted parent as the reason for the child's problems – even if the high-level alienator successfully prevented the alienated parent from having any contact with their child for years.

Detecting Parental Alienation

In an article entitled *Parental Alienation Syndrome: How to Detect It and What to Do About It*, Dr. J. Michael Bone and Dr. Michael R. Walsh point out that diagnosing PAS usually falls within the domain of mental health professionals who testify in court as expert witnesses. As such, according to Bone and Walsh, the experts couch their testimony in clinical terms that are vague and open to interpretation. Bone and Walsh believe that judges have a hard time identifying PAS amid the vague testimony, not to mention the litigants' accusations and counter accusations, associated with most PAS-related custody cases, and have developed four specific criteria for identifying PAS. These criteria remove the accusations, hysteria and hearsay elements from the typical PAS case and focus more on facts that are fairly easy to identify and separate from anything going on inside the courtroom. The four criteria are: *Access and Contact Blocking, Unfounded*

Abuse Allegations, Deterioration in Relationship since Separation and Intense Fear Reaction by Children.

- **Access and Contact Blocking.** Bone and Walsh describe their first criterion for identifying PAS as *the active blocking of access or contact between the child and the absent parent. The rationale used to justify it may well take many different forms. One of the most common is that of protection. It may be argued that the absent parent's parental judgment is inferior and, therefore, the child is much worse off from the visit. In extreme cases, this will take the form of allegations of child abuse, quite often sexual abuse. On a more subtle and common level, an argument heard for the blocking of visitation is that seeing the absent parent is "unsettling" to the child, and that he or she needs time "to adjust." The message here is that the absent parent is treated less like a key family member and more like an annoying acquaintance that the child must see at times. Over time, this pattern can have a seriously erosive effect on the child's relationship with the absent parent. An even more subtle expression of this is that the visitation is "inconvenient." Thereby relegating it to the status of an errand or a chore.*

  The common thread of all of these tactics is that one parent is superior and the other parent is not, and therefore, should be peripheral to the child's life. The alienating parent in these circumstances is acting inappropriately as a gatekeeper for the child to see the absent parent. When this occurs for periods of substantial time, the child is given the unspoken but clear message that one parent is senior to the other.

- **Unfounded Abuse Charges.** *The second criterion is related to false or unfounded accusations of abuse against the absent parent. The most strident expression of this is the false accusation of sexual abuse. It has been well* *studied that false allegations of sexual abuse account for over half of those reported, when the parents are divorcing or are in conflict over some post dissolution issue. This is especially the situation with small children who are more vulnerable to the manipulations implied by such false allegations. When the record shows that even one report of such abuse is ruled unfounded, the interviewer is well advised to look for other expressions of false accusations.*

Bone and Walsh recognized that investigators also find physical abuse allegations unfounded, but not as often as other forms of abuse. Physical abuse leaves visible evidence. It is much easier to falsely accuse someone of something that leaves no physical signs.

However, according to Bone and Walsh, a much more common type of false abuse charge is emotional abuse. *When a false allegation of emotional abuse is leveled, one often finds that what is present is actually differing parental judgment that is being framed as "abusive" by the absent parent. For example, one parent may let a child stay up later at night than the other parent would, and this scheduling might be termed as being "abusive" or "detrimental" to the child. Or one parent might introduce a new "significant other" to the child before the other parent believes that he or she should, and this might also be called "abusive" to the child. These examples, as trivial as they seem individually, may be suggestive of a theme of treating parental differences in inappropriately subjective judgmental terms. If this theme is present, all manners of things can be described in ways that convey the message of abuse, either directly or indirectly. When this phenomenon occurs in literally thousands of different ways and times, each of which seems insignificant on its own, the emotional atmosphere it creates carries a clearly alienating effect on the child.*

Obviously, this type of acrimony is very common in dissolution actions but such conflict should not necessarily be mistaken or taken as illustrative of PAS; however, the criterion is clearly present and identifiable when the parent is eager to hurl abuse allegations, rather than being cautious, careful and even reluctant to do so. This latter stance is more in keeping with the parent's responsibility to encourage and affirmatively support a relationship with the other parent... Simply put, the responsible parent will give the other parent the benefit of the doubt when such allegations arise. He or she will, if anything, err on the side of denial, whereas the alienating parent will not miss an opportunity to accuse the other parent. When this theme is present in a clear and consistent way, this criterion for PAS is met.

- **Deterioration in Relationship since Separation.** According to Bone and Walsh the third criterion is one of the most important of the four PAS criteria – *the breakdown of the once healthy, positive relationship between the child and the alienated parent. Simply put, the relationship does not deteriorate on its own.*

  By way of example, if a father had a good and involved relationship with the child prior to the separation, and a very distant one since, then one can only assume without explicit proof to the contrary that something caused it to change. If this father is clearly trying to maintain a positive relationship with the child through observance of visitation and other activities and the child does not want to see him or have him involved in his or her life, then one can only speculate that an alienation process may have been in operation. A child does not naturally lose interest become distant from the nonresidential parent virtue of the absence of that parent. Also, he established parental relationships do not er their own accord. They must be attacked. T

215

dramatic change in this area is virtually always an indicator of an alienation process that has had some success in the past.

Most notably, if a careful evaluation of the pre-separation parental relationship is not made, its omission creates an impression that the troubled or even alienated status that exists since is more or less an accurate summary of what existed previously. Note that nothing could be further from the truth. An alienated or even partially or intermittently alienated relationship between the nonresidential parent and the child after the separation is more accurately a distortion of the real parental relationship in question.

- **Intense Fear Reaction by Children.** Bone and Walsh's fourth criterion refers to a child's intense fear of displeasing or disagreeing with the alienating parent when it comes to the alienated parent. *Simply put, an alienating parent operates by the adage, "My way or the highway." If the children disobey this directive, especially in expressing positive approval of the absent parent, the consequences can be very serious. It is not uncommon for an alienating parent to reject the child (ren), often telling him or her that they should go live with the target parent. When this does occur one often sees that this threat is not carried out, yet it operates more as a message of constant warning.*

    ... In order to fully appreciate this scenario, one must realize that the PAS process operates in a "fear based" environment. It is the installation of fear by the alienating parent in the minor children that is the fuel by which this pattern is driven; this fear taps into what psychoanalysis tells us is the most basic emotion inherent in human nature – the fear of abandonment. Children under these conditions live in a state of chronic upset and threat of reprisal.

216

In their conclusion, the authors point out that, *when all four criteria are clearly present, and the possibility of real abuse has been reasonably ruled out, the parental alienation process is operative.*

* * * *

Mike: Don't you think a parent on the receiving end of alienating behavior would argue that low or mild parental alienation is never appropriate parenting?

Dr. Davies: Possibly, and the parent would be correct. The identified levels of parental alienation – low, medium and high or mild, moderate and severe – are nothing more than identifying marks or labels along a continuum of behaviors. These labels make it easy for people to clarify and compare the behaviors. Both psychologists and lay people need labels to quickly and easily communicate complicated concepts.

Any parent who places the child's best interests above his or her own is acting contrary to an alienating parent. In reality, low parental alienation isn't alienation at all. I've never met a divorced parent who never made a disparaging comment about the former spouse in front of their child in order to justify the divorce. People naturally use personal pronouns in phrases such as "your father's weekend" or "your mother's house," in order to distinguish between common or similar concepts – "my weekend, my house." Technically, the concept of low parental alienation contradicts the concept of appropriate parenting. But low parental alienation is also appropriate parenting.

Mike: Do low-level alienators typically have any of the emotional or psychological issues we've discussed in the past?

Dr. Davies: Not really. Low-level alienators are separating and individuating themselves from their former lives. They're creating new boundaries for themselves and others – including the former spouse. Emotional issues such as poor object relations, dependency, hysteria or paranoia are probably not playing a role in a low-level alienator's separation and divorce process.

Mike: What happens to a child when one or both parents are low-level alienators?

Dr. Davies: As long as both parents place the child's best interest above their own the child will be fine. As we've discussed, a child is initially devastated when he or she learns Mom and Dad are divorcing and one parent is moving out. Parents help the child through this transition by being consistent, keeping the child out of the divorce, and helping the child incorporate the new reality into his or her world.

Mike: What can a psychologist do for a child in this situation?

Dr. Davies: A psychologist can help a child express feelings of loss, sadness and anger. Children go through their own stages of loss and it's important to talk with them in ways that are appropriate for their ages.

          A younger child may be confused and unable to speak about how he feels. The child may feel the divorce is his fault. This child needs clear and consistent messages that the divorce is not his fault, Mom and Dad still love him and will continue to take care of him.

Adolescents and teenagers are much more vocal and able to speak about how they feel. They're also more likely to develop emotional problems. Children this age can turn to drugs and alcohol as coping mechanisms. Adolescents and teenagers need to keep busy. They shouldn't isolate themselves from their normal routines. In fact, the less change to their routines the better. Like younger children, these kids need to know everything will be okay.

Mike: How serious are the medium-level alienator's emotional problems?

Dr. Davies: Emotional issues drive the medium-level alienator's inappropriate behavior. A medium-level alienator or reactive alienating parent will tend to have more emotional issues present than someone who falls into the low-level alienator category. These parents have the ability to emotionally regroup after a blow-up. They inflict some emotional damage on the child and the other parent but they help heal the rift, because when the anger subsides they recognize that good relationships with both parents are in the child's best interest.

Mike: How can a psychologist help a medium-level alienator quickly get past the anger and regain control?

Dr. Davies: A psychologist can help the medium-level alienator realize that his or her feelings are normal. Getting past the anger may take time. In the meantime, a good clinician will advise the person to take care through diet, exercise, social and recreational activities. It sounds simplistic, but staying busy is an excellent way to deal appropriately with anger. A person with a full schedule and challenging activities simply doesn't have the time or energy to stay angry.

Unfortunately, a person can stay extremely busy and still occasionally feel the anger building up inside. At those times the person needs a good emotional support system in place – including someone to talk to – so that when he or she feels the anger building the individual can talk about the feelings causing the anger. A person could even keep a journal as a way to purge negative feelings.

Mike: How can a psychologist help a child get through the highs and lows of living with a medium-level alienator?

Dr. Davies: There isn't much difference between how a psychologist approaches a child living with a low-level alienator and a child living with a medium-level alienator. In both low- and medium-level cases the psychologist tries to help the child re-establish a sense of security, consistency and a new reality. However, every time one parent bashes or denigrates the other parent in front of the child it delays this process.

Because a medium-level alienator or reactive alienating parent will act out more than a low-level alienating parent, the child of a medium-level alienator is exposed to the behavior more often. At these times the child will feel conflicted. There isn't much a psychologist can do to help the child avoid feeling conflicted. An older, more independent child with better developed verbal skill can either avoid the medium-level alienating parent during these episodes or tell the parent that listening to negative comments about the other parent is very painful. But the psychologist's main role in these cases would be to work with the child and parents together during sessions to make sure the parents know how their comments and actions affect the child.

Mike: What advice do you have for an alienated parent who is on the receiving end of a medium-level alienator's outbursts?

Dr. Davies: Don't play the same game. Don't act the same way. An alienated parent may be doing things that repeatedly cause a reaction in the other parent. The parent should be aware of how his or her actions evoke specific responses from the alienating parent.

There isn't much an alienated parent can do to control an ex-spouse's reaction. But when the medium-level alienating parent responds inappropriately, the other parent should get out of the situation if the ex-spouse can't regain control. Once the ex-spouse does regain control, the alienated parent can always revisit the issue and try to resolve the conflict – after first making sure the child isn't within earshot of the conversation.

Mike: Can a high-level alienator ever change?

Dr. Davies: Theoretically, a high-level alienator can change. Practically, this person doesn't want to change.

In order to change his or her behavior a high-level alienator would have to make a tremendous commitment to get the necessary help. This means that the alienator would have to come face-to-face with all his or her unresolved emotional issues. A high-level alienator isn't willing to make that commitment. Remember, in this parent's mind, he or she is the perfect parent. The other parent is always at fault. An alienating parent consistently avoids any thought or action that would reflect negatively on his or her perception of him or herself as the perfect parent. This parent finds it much easier to blame someone else.

The high-level alienator feels such an intense level of betrayal and abandonment that the parent's main mission becomes revenge and the destruction of a relationship that was loved and cherished by the other parent. This parent isn't going to change.

Mike: What advice do you have for an alienated parent who is on the receiving end of a high-level alienator's campaign of denigration?

Dr. Davies: Keep calm. Don't react or respond. Don't come across as a hot-head or as an explosive personality. An alienated parent must anticipate that the high-level alienator will fabricate situations designed to evoke a reaction. Don't be caught off guard. I find it more than a little ironic that paranoia is one of the psychological elements that can contribute to severe parental alienation; however a healthy dose of paranoia is exactly what an alienated parent needs to protect him or herself from a high-level alienator's need for revenge.

13

The Attorneys' Roles

WHEN I WAS INTERVIEWING ATTORNEYS prior to selecting the one who would ultimately represent me in court, I ran across one attorney who gave me more insight into divorce and the legal process than all the other attorneys combined:

> *"Divorce isn't about two people getting divorced. Divorce is about four people getting divorced. There are the two people who were married and their two new attorney/partners. Any one of the four can screw up the divorce at any time."*

In a high conflict divorce and child custody case, the court may also appoint an attorney to represent the minor child's wishes. The court may even appoint a second attorney – a Guardian Ad Litem – to represent the child's best interests. At this point, according to the above-quoted attorney's theory, there is a minimum of seven people uniquely qualified to screw up the divorce – at a billing rate of hundreds of dollars an hour per attorney.

Most attorneys don't deliberately screw up the process. Attorneys represent their clients' best interests to the best of their abilities. Their goal is to win the battle – and their clients define what "winning" means. Money, property and children are generally what divorcing parents, and therefore their attorneys, fight over. Both sides measure success by how much they can take away, or keep, from the previously loved spouse.

In a divorce and child custody case involving severe parental alienation, an alienating parent may have already won before ever entering a courtroom if he or she has successfully destroyed the child's previously loving relationship with the other parent. When the parent does enter the courtroom with his or her attorney, the alienating parent fights to maintain the status quo and keep the alienated parent away from the child. The attorney does his or her best to represent the client's wishes. On the other side of the courtroom, the alienated parent fights desperately to make up lost ground and re-establish his or her role in the child's life. This parent's attorney does his or her best to represent the targeted parent's wishes. Somewhere else in the courtroom is the attorney for the minor child and maybe even a Guardian Ad Litem. They do their best to succeed on behalf of their client.

Each attorney also comes to court to satisfy his or her own internally driven needs. One attorney is probably in the profession for the money. Another attorney might enjoy the power that goes with altering other peoples' lives. A third attorney relishes the "fight" and the thrill of victory. A fourth likes helping people. Most attorneys enjoy their work for the equal parts of money, power, the thrill of victory and the ability to help others. An alienated parent must understand each attorney's motivation, role and responsibilities if he or she hopes to regain a relationship with the child. Understanding the attorneys, even the soon-to-be ex-spouse's attorney, is the key to making good decisions that will ultimately affect everyone's future.

The Alienated Parent's Attorney

People tend to gravitate towards other people who share backgrounds, values and philosophies similar to their own. Both personally and professionally, we all feel most comfortable with people who remind us of ourselves.

I interviewed three attorneys before selecting one to represent me. The first attorney said, "You'll get screwed." The second attorney said, "We'll screw her." The third attorney, Lisa Slater, said, "I won't let you get screwed, but I won't represent you if you expect me to help you screw her."

Lisa practiced something called, "Collaborative Law." Collaborative Law is a process where the attorneys for both parties in a family dispute bypass the adversarial techniques and typical litigation options common to most family law cases in favor of cooperative strategies designed to resolve the conflicts with dignity and civility. Attorneys who practice Collaborative Law use skills such as analysis, facilitation, creative thinking and problem solving to create a positive environment that leads to a settlement rather than a trial.

During the interview Lisa asked, "Will child custody be an issue?" "No," I responded naively. At the time I fully expected Beth would support joint legal and physical custody of both children. I imagined Beth and me cooperating with each other so Jared and Adam could move back and forth between our households with as little stress and inconvenience as possible. I was still months away from filing for divorce. Despite Beth's clear signals, I had no idea that my post-divorce plans would bear little resemblance to my post-divorce reality. Lisa's talk about reaching a fair and equitable agreement without the time and expense of the normal adversarial process matched perfectly with the rose-colored glasses I was wearing.

Attorney Slater also had something else going for her that the other two attorneys didn't. She was, how should I say this, nice. I liked her. We shared some things in common – a Jewish heritage, background in photography and an interest in exercise. She was also a good listener, empathetic and caring. Lisa reminded me of some of my friends. Hell, sometimes she reminded me of me.

In retrospect, Lisa was a great choice for me, but maybe not the best choice for my case. Facilitation, creative thinking and problem solving are often fruitless exercises in a severe case of parental alienation. Fair is a wonderful concept, but the alienating parent doesn't fight by the Marquess of Queensberry rules. I often wonder if I would have been better served if I had invited Lisa and her husband out to dinner, and then hired the attorney who was ready to go after Beth for the fun of it.

How could Lisa be a bad choice for my case when the judge gave us everything we asked for as it related to the kids? Because by the time the judge issued his orders with respect to Adam, his orders were meaningless and unenforceable.

Time is the alienating parent's best weapon. The longer he or she can keep the alienated parent away from the child, the tougher it will be for the parent and child to rebuild their previously loving and healthy relationship. In the child's everyday life of school, friends and activities, out of sight is out of mind. In addition, the only references the child will hear concerning the previously loved parent are negative references. Since the child's positive feelings about the parent have been replaced with negative ones, he or she has no trouble adjusting to life without the previously loved parent.

Instead of an attorney who practices Collaborative Law, a severely alienated parent might be better off with an aggressive attorney skilled in the adversarial elements of the judicial process. This attorney will throw away the normal timeline for resolving divorce and child custody issues in favor of a calendar where hours become minutes, days become hours and weeks become days. Whether the issue is returning a phone call or complying with a court order, the aggressive attorney doesn't give the alienating parent and his or her attorney one extra inch, or more appropriately, one extra second. This attorney would just as soon file a motion for another appearance before the judge as reach a fair and equitable agreement in a civil environment.

I also wonder if my case suffered because Lisa suffered from what I call the "too" disease.

Lisa may have been too fair, too nice, too courteous and too empathetic for my case. I believe she waited too patiently for the other attorneys or the court-appointed psychologist involved in my case to return her calls. Days would pass without a call until I harassed her into calling back and harassing the other professionals into moving faster. She was too non-confrontational to use contempt motions. Lisa thought filing contempt motions against Beth would backfire and the judge would think I was a bully. She was too worried about Adam – worried that pushing too hard would further upset my already emotionally troubled son. She gave the other professionals in my case too much credit – expecting them to reach the same "correct" conclusions she reached. Most of all, she was just too much like me. Maybe I needed an attorney to protect me from myself, not reinforce my naive view of how the world, and everyone in it, should operate?

For example, one time Beth's third attorney asked if we could reschedule a Monday status conference so he wouldn't have to rush back from his daughter's out-of-town wedding. Lisa called and asked me what I wanted to do. I said, "Of course we should reschedule the status conference. His daughter is getting married. Besides, we might need a similar courtesy one day." She agreed. The status conference was put off for weeks.

Once I thought about switching attorneys. I called someone known for being ruthless – just the opposite of Lisa's reputation. But at one point during the conversation this attorney suggested I stop paying the mortgage on the house. Let the bank foreclose, she said. I was appalled. She was talking about my children's home. I could never do anything like that. I went running back to my fair, empathetic attorney. Lisa would never suggest anything that would hurt my kids.

But I have to wonder – an attorney who counsels a client to let the bank foreclose on the severely alienated child's home might be exactly the kind of tough, my-way-or-the-highway kind of attorney that gets everyone moving. Perhaps a severely alienated parent's best strategy is to hire this type of attorney and get out of the way. The attorney probably wouldn't offer the extra courtesies Lisa provided – such as the handholding, friendship, and daily reassurance that she was on the job. But in the final analysis a successful attorney doesn't have to show his or her client any more courtesy than the attorney shows the alienating parent. If the alienated parent hires the right attorney, he or she will let the attorney do his or her job and trust the attorney will do that job better than the other attorneys do their jobs.

Lisa really cared. And she tried hard. She thought about my case constantly – when she was watching television, driving and spending time with her own children. She returned every one of my calls and read and responded to hundreds of my emails. But Lisa wasn't willing to do whatever was necessary to prevent Beth from getting the time she needed to make the alienation irreversible. If Lisa's approach was different Adam may have suffered more in the short-term, but perhaps his long-term outlook would be much brighter.

The Alienating Parent's Attorney

The alienating parent also selects an attorney who shares values and a philosophy similar to his or her values and philosophy. The last thing this parent wants is for the formerly loved spouse to rebuild a relationship with their child. He or she won't cooperate or compromise on any issue that could potentially bring the alienated parent and child together. So it only makes sense that he or she will hire an attorney who doesn't cooperate or compromise either.

If hysteria, paranoia and psychopathic behavior are characteristics of an alienating parent, then it stands to reason that the alienating parent will look for an attorney who is also prone, or at least sympathetic to, hysteria, paranoia and psychopathic behavior. Law is a profession where many of its practitioners zealously defend the rights of David against Goliath. Controlled hysterical/dramatic outbursts in the courtroom; a healthy dose of paranoia toward people out to discredit you and your position; and manipulation without any shame, guilt or empathy for the people you're hurting are all common commodities in the legal profession.

The key phrase in the last paragraph, and with many attorneys, is "zealously defend." The alienating parent pays his or her attorney to zealously defend his or her position. The attorney ignores or discredits anything that doesn't support the alienating parent's position and highlights and even exaggerates anything that helps the alienating parent. Truth, or more accurately the attorney's perception of the truth, is often irrelevant.

The attorney's Rules of Professional Conduct back up this approach. The Rules state that the attorney's task is to present the client's case with persuasive force. However, an attorney does not vouch for the evidence he or she submits to the court. The Rules also state that the attorney doesn't have to believe his or her representations to the court. The attorney can represent anything as long as he or she doesn't know for a fact that the representation is a lie. That's why Beth's third attorney prefaced all his comments with phrases such as, "My client tells me…" or "According to my client…" What these qualifying statements really meant was, "I'm about to distort the hell out of something my client told me. I'm not sure if I even believe it myself. However my job is to advocate my client's position and portray that position in the best possible light. It's the court's job to decide what's true and what's not true."

It took Beth three tries to hit the attorney trifecta of hysteria, paranoia and psychopathic behavior. Her first attorney just acted hysterical. At least I think he was acting. He wasn't her attorney long enough to find out for sure. On our very first day in court I was standing towards the front of the courthouse when I heard a booming voice from the back of the building. The booming voice was yelling about a horrible husband who constantly denigrated his wife. The speaker became more agitated by the second. I walked towards the back of the courthouse. The story was getting juicy and I couldn't hear a single response from whomever the guy was yelling at. I must have walked 100 feet when I finally got close enough to hear someone respond. That someone was my attorney. I was the horrible husband and Beth was the denigrated wife.

Beth's second attorney wasn't really prone to hysterical behavior. And I believe she had empathy for Jared and Adam. She was Beth's attorney when we developed the parenting agreement that allowed Jared to split his time between the two households and had Adam in therapy. We went to trial because Beth and her third attorney backed out of this agreement. But Beth's second attorney appeared to buy into Beth's baseless accusations a little too enthusiastically. Did attorney number two possess a healthy dose of occupational paranoia or was she just following up on her client's requests to the best of her ability (and at a billing rate of a couple of hundred dollars per hour)?

I'll never know the answer, but I do know Beth's second attorney spent a lot of time calling my attorney and writing letters that supported Beth's ongoing character attacks. One time Beth, through her attorney, accused me of breaking into the house and stealing important papers. Another time they accused me of stealing the computer from the house. Beth wasn't even smart enough to get rid of the computer before saying I took it. The day that accusation arrived, Jared confirmed the computer was sitting where it always sat. Finally Lisa told them to call the police, and not her, next time they think something is missing from the house. Predictably, that comment put an end to any further breaking and entering allegations.

I can only imagine that Beth fired her first two attorneys because they didn't tell her what she wanted to hear. Attorneys give their clients advice. However the clients often want to make the decisions. An alienating parent operates in a very black and white world. If the attorney gives the alienating parent the advice he or she wants to hear, the attorney is a trusted, knowledgeable, white-hat-wearing, good guy. If the attorney gives advice contrary to what the alienating parent wants to hear, the alienating parent starts suspecting the attorney's motives and credibility. Too much "wrong" advice and the attorney becomes a black-hat-wearing, bad guy. This attorney also becomes history.

Beth's third attorney possessed all the qualities I believe Beth wanted in an attorney – equal parts hysteria, paranoia and the ability to manipulate situations without shame, guilt or empathy for anyone.

Attorney number three showed up late for court-ordered appearances, and three times he didn't show up at all. The attorney's first no-show act was his first day on the case. He failed to appear for a long-scheduled status conference to discuss Adam's deteriorating emotional health. He later told the judge he was absent because he was on trial in another courtroom. Three weeks later the judge admonished him on the record. "Attorneys accept cases at their own peril," the judge said sternly. Big deal. The damage was long done. The judge wouldn't proceed without Beth's attorney present on the day of the original status conference. Beth gained another three weeks.

When Beth's third attorney did arrive at court, he spent hours "meeting" with his client – making the rest of us cool our heels. When he couldn't delay going before the judge any longer, he expertly talked about anything other than the issues before the court. He made sure the judge didn't have time to address any issue related to Adam's therapy or my court-ordered time with him – forcing everyone to return to court at a later date and watch him successfully use the same delay tactics again.

When Beth's attorney launched into one of his patented monologues, he hammered home key points that he wanted to reinforce at every opportunity. He wanted to convince the judge that I was a lying cheat, an unfit parent and a menace to society. No matter what question the judge asked, no matter what topic the other attorneys were discussing, Beth's attorney responded with a litany of false allegations and fictional accounts that hammered home his three points. I got the feeling that if the judge asked the attorney how his children were enjoying summer camp, the attorney would have launched into his auto-pilot response and inadvertently accused his own kids of being lying cheats, unfit parents and menaces to society.

This guy also wasn't above ignoring the law if ignoring the law helped his client. On one occasion I listened as the judge asked him if there were any legal precedent, anywhere, for what he asked the judge to order. Clearly, the judge knew there wasn't any precedent. And after watching Beth's attorney tap dance around the judge's question for 20 minutes, I'm pretty sure everyone else in the courtroom knew there wasn't any precedent. Finally, the judge forced the attorney to admit there was no legal basis for what he asked for on his client's behalf.

A common mistake among alienated parents is to expect the alienating parent's attorney to have empathy for the child involved in the case. At the end of the day, the alienated parent reasons, many attorneys are parents. Parenthood, a love for our children, and a heartfelt desire to protect our children from harm are the common ties that bind us together. Sure, the alienated parent further reasons, I expect the attorney to do the best he or she can for my soon-to-be ex. But I also expect that the attorney wouldn't deliberately hurt the child.

What the alienated parent doesn't understand is that the alienating parent's attorney does not share his or her perception of what's best for the child. The attorney is paid to represent what the alienating parent believes is best for the child. The attorney's personal views, if he or she even bothers expending the mental energy to develop personal views, are irrelevant. If the attorney wants to stay on the case, he or she will strongly advocate the alienating parent's position. An attorney responsible for worrying about what's best for the child is called a Guardian Ad Litem.

The Child's Attorney and the Guardian Ad Litem

The minute a judge smells a potential custody battle; he or she may begin looking for the child's legal representation. After all, the judge reasons, both parents have attorneys representing their positions. Who is representing the child's position? An attorney for a minor child ensures that neither parent manipulates the child's interests before the court.

A child's attorney is the child's advocate in court – just as an adult's attorney is the adult's advocate. An attorney representing a child can call witnesses; cross-examine the other side's witnesses and file motions on their client's behalf.

A Guardian Ad Litem (GAL) could be an attorney, but doesn't have to be an attorney. The GAL stands in the shoes of the child before the court. This person doesn't represent to the court what the child wants, but what is in the child's best interest. Much like the other litigants, the GAL is a witness or party to the proceedings. If the GAL wants to ask a question, he or she will typically go through the child's attorney. That's right, even when the GAL is an attorney, the attorney for the child will speak for the

GAL in the courtroom. One of the few exceptions to this rule is when a GAL files a pro se appearance. A pro se appearance allows a litigant, any litigant, to represent him or herself in court without an attorney. Of course, an attorney acting as a GAL for a child can file a pro se appearance. Then the attorney, theoretically standing in the shoes of the child, will represent the child's best interest to the court.

Phil Crawford started as Jared and Adam's attorney, and became their GAL shortly before the trial when Adam forced Crawford to represent a position to the court that no one, except Beth, thought was in Adam's best interests. Since Adam's refusal to see me, talk to me, or attend therapy sessions was so well documented, the judge agreed to let Crawford, as GAL, file a pro se appearance. Crawford began representing Jared and Adam's best interests rather than their wishes.

I was never very comfortable with Crawford's approach to Jared and Adam. Of course, I didn't have any prior experience with an attorney representing my children, but when Crawford gave Jared his business card and said, "Call me if you need anything," I thought something wasn't quite right. Shouldn't Crawford have been the one calling Jared and Adam once in a while to see how they were doing? Shouldn't he have at least tried to win their trust so they would be comfortable talking to him? But Crawford worked with his under-age clients the same way attorneys work with their adult clients – at arm's length. What child will call a stranger, a court-appointed stranger no less, when that stranger represents everything the child is upset about, i.e., his parent's divorce?

I also thought Crawford should have questioned Beth's uncooperative behavior more. If he wondered why Beth rarely returned his phone calls, or called back after office hours with a, "sorry I missed you" message, he never said anything. Nor did he question why a stay-at-home Mom often cancelled Adam's appointments at the last minute – and then couldn't reschedule the appointment for a date less than three weeks away. When Beth told Crawford, "I'll have to ask my attorney," or, "I'll discuss it with Adam and get back to you," in response to just about any request, did Crawford really understand that Beth was saying, "I'm resisting your idea and not telling you so you can't call me uncooperative in front of the judge?" Of course, Beth never got back to her children's attorney, and Crawford never called her uncooperative, at least not in the courtroom.

* * * *

Mike: I need to talk to an attorney about divorce and child custody cases.

Ron Griffin: Are you looking for representation? I primarily represent children and act as a Guardian Ad Litem in contested divorce and child custody cases. I'm not the best person to represent you, but I could refer you to someone else in our firm.

Mike: No, I'm not looking for representation. My divorce is over. My younger son and I are victims of parental alienation. I'm on this quest to understand what happened to us and why it happened. My therapist has been a big help but when I started talking about my experiences with the legal system he suggested I get a legal perspective. In particular, I wasn't happy with my children's attorney, who later became their GAL.

Ron Griffin: I'm familiar with parental alienation. Those are the toughest cases. However, as the attorney for the child or the guardian, if I do my job properly the case never goes before the judge. It's my job to protect the child from the conflict by helping the parents reach an agreement. I'm not successful in every case, but my goal is to protect my client.

Mike: In a severe case of parental alienation, you always have an alienating parent who will not cooperate under any circumstance.

Ron Griffin: That's why alienation cases are the hardest cases. I tell parents all the time, "Whether the reasons for the divorce are correct or not, you two are responsible for wrecking your child's family. You two are also responsible for making it as easy as possible for him or her." Unfortunately, an alienating parent never listens.

Mike: How does an attorney representing a child gain the child's trust?

Ron Griffin: That depends on the child's age. When I work with a pre-school child, I never meet the child in my office. I go to the child's house wearing jeans and a sweater and I get down on the floor and play with him or her. During the first visit or two, I don't usually ask about Mom, Dad or the divorce. Besides, you can't ask a toddler a direct question such as, "Where do you want to live?" A child that young doesn't have the cognitive ability to answer questions like that logically. That's why, with very young children, attorneys should obtain information from other people involved in the child's life. People such as the day care workers, the pediatrician, the therapist, the extended family members and friends are all excellent sources of information about the child.

My approach is the same with an adolescent – I try to establish a relationship with the child. I go to the child's home, attend soccer games and school programs, and show an interest in the child's hobbies. After a couple of visits I begin asking gentle questions such as, "How are things at school? How are things at home? Do you feel that both your parents listen to you? Do you have any concerns about the divorce? Anything you want me to discuss with Mom and Dad for you?"

I also explain to an adolescent client the significance of having an attorney. "You're the boss, and I have to tell the court what you want," I say. Young kids get a big kick out of that. Of course, if my client tries to fire me, I also point out that as quickly as I'm gone another attorney will take my place, and no attorney will do what a child says if the child is unreasonable. An adolescent is generally mature enough to understand a reality check.

The hardest child to represent is a teenager. Teenagers typically think they are Supermen and Superwomen – bulletproof masters of the universe who don't need anyone. For these kids, even in happy two parent households, Mom and Dad often only exist as ATM machines and taxi drivers.

A teenager going through his or her parent's divorce is usually much angrier than a younger child. The teenager takes the divorce personally. After all, the divorcing parents are inconveniencing the child, messing up his or her life. A teenager will really push the envelope during a high-conflict divorce. The child will use the natural rebellion that occurs at that age and take it to the next level. The teen feels his or her anger empowers him or her to act out.

Mike: Do you set boundaries with your under-age clients? After all, you're not a $200-an-hour playmate or big brother.

Ron Griffin: I do set boundaries, but boundaries are harder with kids. An attorney must be more flexible with children than adults.

For example, I'll give a child my home phone number. I'll also give a child more of my personal time. I'll see a child on the weekend because he or she is in school when I'm typically working.

An attorney must be vigilant when it comes to boundaries and remind the child that the attorney is there to help, but the child still must listen to Mom and Dad. Having an attorney doesn't mean the child is excused from doing what he or she is supposed to do.

Mike: Do children really call you?

Ron Griffin: They really do call. If I do my job correctly they see me as an advocate and friend. They'll call me and say, "I can't take it. You have to help me."

Mike: How often do you get nonsense calls and how do you handle your clients then?

Ron Griffin: Twenty-five or thirty percent of the calls fall into the category of, "Mom or Dad won't let me stay up late." Then I tell my client what my parents told me – "You're acting like a spoiled brat. Go to bed."

Mike: What is the biggest challenge when working with your client's parents?

Ron Griffin: The biggest challenge is convincing parents to listen to their child. Parents need to stop being mad, stop blaming the spouse and listen to their child. This challenge becomes even bigger when one parent is unreasonable and demands a specific result. That's when the unreasonable parent usually says to me, "Why are you letting a nine-year-old child have a vote?"

Mike: Good question. Why are you letting a nine-year-old child have a vote?

Ron Griffin: Because I believe that a little person is allowed to have some autonomy in his or her feelings, and adults should respect those feelings. If parents are unwilling to listen to their child and consider the child's feelings they really aren't helping the child through a difficult time.

Mike: What happens when the nine year old says, "I never want to talk to Mom? I never want to see Mom again?"

Ron Griffin: That depends on how entrenched the child is in his or her position. I once represented a nine-year-old girl who didn't want to talk or see her Mom. Mom left this nine year old and was living with another man and a new baby. But the child's position wasn't very entrenched. When I asked her if she would ever want Mom to fix her hair, help pick out a prom dress or walk down the aisle at her wedding, I saw the tears start to form in her eyes. After two or three months my client finally admitted that I had a point.

Mike: What about an alienated child who remains steadfast in his or her refusal to have a relationship with the alienated parent?

Ron Griffin: A child should not be empowered to the point where he or she thinks being an alienated child is a good thing. As the child's attorney I have an obligation to go to court and articulate what the child wants. However, if I believe what the child wants is not in his or her best interest, I tell the child I don't agree, and while I'll continue representing that position to the court, I'll also ask the court to appoint a GAL. Then I can question the GAL about what is in the child's best interest.

Mike: Is the GAL typically an attorney?

Ron Griffin: In my state the GAL is typically an attorney. Other states appoint GALs from a variety of professions. I believe children would be better served if more mental health professionals functioned as guardians.

Mike: If you are a GAL do you approach a case differently than if you are the attorney for the child?

Ron Griffin: The role of the GAL is to act as the body of the child in the courtroom.

Technically the GAL is not supposed to speak in court unless he or she files a pro se appearance. If there is a GAL, nine times out of ten there is also an attorney for the minor child. If I'm a guardian and I want to ask a witness a question at the trial, I write the question down on a little piece of paper and pass it to the attorney.

Mike: When most lay people hear the word guardian they don't think of a person whose only role is to speak for the child in court. They think of a guardian as someone who makes sure the child goes to school, does his or her homework, and gets the child to the doctor when the child has an appointment. Are those responsibilities also part of a GALs role?

Ron Griffin: Yes, a GAL does have some obligation to do all those things. There are times when a GAL must act like a parent. If a child isn't going to school, the GAL should go to the parents and say, "If the child doesn't go to school, I will send someone over to take the child to school."

Mike: What are the limitations of a GAL?

Ron Griffin: For me the biggest limitation is my training as an attorney. I'm trained to go to court and participate in the legal process. When the court asks a legal professional to become a GAL, the court is essentially asking the attorney to become a parent. But we don't have the proper background to deal with someone else's child and really serve the child's best interests. Attorneys are not psychiatrists or psychologists. We don't have the tools to figure out what really motivates a child.

                That's why when I'm representing a child my most important contact is the mental health professional. If there is no mental health professional involved in my case, and it becomes painfully clear that there needs to be one, then I'll make a motion to get a mental health professional involved. Attorneys rely on these professionals to be the experts.

Mike: Do you ever clash with the mental health professionals involved in your cases?

Ron Griffin: Clashes occur because both attorneys and parents want definite answers and instant gratification. Definite answers and instant gratification are two things mental health professionals never give us. As the attorney I say, "You can get this done in four weeks." The mental health professional says, "No way. I need four months."

Another clash occurs when the mental health professional says the ongoing legal conflict is part of the child's problem. Well, that may be true, but as the attorney I'm part of the ongoing conflict. An attorney must advocate his or her client's position to the best of his or her ability. That responsibility often conflicts with the mental health professional's recommendation to end the hostilities as quickly as possible for the sake of the child.

14

How Courts Botch Parental Alienation Cases

BEFORE JUDGE JUDY or any other retired judge started dispensing televised justice in 22 entertainment-filled minutes, I remember a show called *Divorce Court*.

I don't remember much about the show. I do remember the show came on every afternoon at 4:00 p.m. And I remember my mother usually turned the television off every afternoon at 4:02 p.m. No way will my child watch that piece of garbage, she always said.

On those rare occasions when I was able to watch the entire show undetected, I was young enough to believe that two people could actually get divorced in the time it took Mom to make dinner. I don't remember if child custody was ever an issue on *Divorce Court* -- probably not. In the 1960s the common understanding was that children of divorce would live with Mom and visit Dad.

Having spent the better part of the last two years in real Divorce Court, also known as family court in many states, I can tell you that nothing in court gets resolved in 30 minutes. The wheels of justice don't even begin turning in such a short amount of time. I can also tell you that many judges probably wish their cases were as easy to dispose of as the fictional cases I used to watch on television. Most judges view parental alienation as an unwanted complication to what is usually an already messy divorce and child custody battle.

Judges who preside over family court preside over "Courts of Equitable Distribution." The word "equitable" implies that all people before the court will be treated equally in accordance with the law. The word "distribution" implies these courts will divide or parcel out the family assets when the primary family members are unable to reach an agreement on their own. Put the two concepts together and you might logically conclude that family courts divide family assets equally between people in accordance with the law.

If you reached that logical conclusion, you would be partially correct. Most judges know how to split up bank accounts and personal property. However, they don't know what to do in child custody cases or even joint custody situations when a young child refuses to have any contact with one parent, and that parent accuses the other parent of destroying the previously loving parent/child bond.

The first problem is that family courts, like all courts in the United States, are based on the adversarial system of justice – a system that gives both sides the opportunity to confront each other before an impartial judge or jury. Each side presents its arguments, witnesses and evidence while doing its best to discredit the arguments, witnesses and evidence of the other side. One family court judge was fond of saying that he could spot insincerity and lies from a mile away. He warned the attorneys and the litigants not to try and put anything over on him. The judge's admonition contradicted the entire premise of family court – a premise based on using whatever means necessary to outwit and discredit the other side in front of the judge. Insincerity, half-truths and lies of omission are standard operating procedure in family court.

This same judge once said, "Numbers don't lie, people do." Unfortunately, there are very few numbers in parental alienation cases. There are only people – mothers, fathers and children. One parent is fighting to keep the other parent out of the child's life. The other parent is fighting to get back into the child's life. Each parent is fighting for the future of his or her most cherished possession – the child. One parent, maybe both parents, will lie. One parent, maybe both parents, will bend or break courtroom rules designed to protect the integrity of the proceedings. One parent, maybe both parents, will fail to realize that the very system they turned to in order to resolve their differences is responsible for increasingly hostile acts that raise the levels of anger, bitterness and distrust between the parties. These acts ultimately prolong the proceedings at huge financial and emotional costs to all parties. Finally, one parent, maybe both parents, will fail to recognize the destructive impact the proceedings have on the child. The one person both parties are trying desperately to protect at any cost ultimately gets lost in the shuffle. The case becomes more about winning and less about the child's best interests.

And who gets to sort it all out? A judge.

In fairness to judges everywhere, today's litigious society has created far too many attorneys and litigants looking to use the legal process in order to make money at someone else's expense. These people create such a backlog of cases on a daily basis that a judge can't possibly spend more than a few minutes on each case. A judge's primary goal each time he or she dons that black robe is to dispose of as many cases as possible as quickly as possible.

In pursuit of that goal, the judge encourages attorneys and litigants to reach an agreement on their own without the court's involvement. The judge relies on court "family relations counselors" or special court-sanctioned mediators and arbitration programs to help the combatants reach an agreement without taking up valuable court, a.k.a. judicial, time.

Unfortunately, an alienating parent isn't interested in reaching any kind of agreement that would allow the other parent back in the alienated child's life. Together with his or her attorney, the parent delays the proceedings in order to frustrate any chance the alienated parent has of rebuilding a relationship with the child. The alienating parent also ignores court counselors' suggestions and court orders that could potentially repair the damaged parent/child relationship. If the alienated parent has money to keep fighting for his or her child, the case inevitably ends up back in the judge's lap. A judge has the power to answer all the alienated parent's prayers or squash any chance he or she may have of ever having a normal, healthy relationship with the child. More often than not the judge is the unwitting carpenter who hammers the final nail into the coffin that was the previously loving parent/child relationship.

Why? Let's start with the judge's ego. A judge can't help but have a huge ego. He sits on a raised platform all day long looking down – literally and sometimes figuratively – on the people who come before the court. He is the final arbitrator on matters of law and no one dares question his authority, judgment or wisdom. A family court judge has the last word on human relationships. He tells divorcing parents how much time each parent can spend with his or her own children. He can even tell a divorcing couple how to split up their pots and pans. Who wouldn't have a huge ego in that situation?

Once, when an attorney tried introducing a motion that the judge in my case wasn't scheduled to hear, the judge lectured the attorney on the differences between a delicatessen and a courtroom.

In a deli, the judge explained, people can select from a variety of items displayed in the refrigerated case. "Court does not offer variety," he said. "Attorneys are required to stick to the motions before the bench." The judge went to great lengths to distinguish between lunchmeats and motions. He took great relish, no pun intended, in dressing down the attorney in much the same manner that the John Houseman character in *The Paper Chase* used to embarrass his law school students. The judge's lecture lasted so long I wondered if his honor was going to offer the attorney a pickle and a choice of white, whole wheat or rye bread with the admonition.

Unfortunately, any judge who goes to such great lengths to embarrass an attorney in court has much too big an ego to ever really understand parental alienation.

Judges like the deli judge often believe they've seen it all and heard it all. If a judge hasn't faced a specific situation from his perch in the courtroom, he has his long experience as an attorney to fall back on. The first time my attorney described Beth's alienating behavior as parental alienation, the judge sneered, "I see that stuff go on all the time." I could literally hear the sarcasm dripping from his lips.

The truth is many judges have seen alienating behavior throughout their careers. Recognizing the symptoms is easy. I'm sure doctors in the 1970s and early 1980s recognized flu-like symptoms -- fever, headaches, nausea and vomiting – without understanding that their patient had AIDS. But much like doctors can't treat a patient without understanding what causes the symptoms, judges can't effectively issue orders in alienation cases without understanding what drives the alienating parent and the alienated child to act the way they do.

A judge may mentally dismiss accusations of alienating behavior as just normal posturing on the part of the litigant. In the judge's mind, every litigant is attempting to promote the favorable outcome of his or her case. The judge believes his or her job is to see through such obvious posturing and hyperbole. So the judge takes the alienation accusations with a grain of salt. Instead of paying close attention to the accusations, trying to understand what motivates the behavior and coming up with a decision to address the problem, the judge mentally relates this new courtroom experience to similar courtroom experiences from his past. Then the judge renders a decision based less on new information and more on past experiences.

In today's courtrooms, judges are unlikely to spend the time it takes to really understand parental alienation – even when listening to testimony from court-appointed psychologists or expert witnesses. For one thing, the concept of parental alienation is relatively new. Gardner only coined the term in the 1980s. Alienated parents are just beginning to introduce parental alienation as a family dynamic that needs the attention of the court. A judge routinely issues decisions based on case law that goes back decades. At this time the concept of parental alienation is too new for most judges. They're not ready to give alienation serious legal weight in their courtrooms. I can imagine a judge thinking, "Let someone write some case law on this first. Then I'll consider it in my ruling."

Many judges consider parental alienation nothing more than a combination of two embattled spouses with an axe to grind and bad parenting. They hold the view that the best place to address the issue is in a mental health professional's office and not a courtroom. They're right. But what most judges typically don't understand, or don't want to understand, is that getting everyone to cooperate with the professional in a timely fashion is a judge's job. They're the only person with the power and authority to put the alienated child in the therapist's office.

Parental alienation cases need quick and decisive action. A therapist only has a small window of opportunity to reach an alienated child before the child's alienated position becomes entrenched and irreversible. When a judge issues an order, he expects the parties will follow the order immediately and without question. In order to impress upon everyone in the courtroom how serious he is about his order, a judge will talk sternly to litigants. "There will be severe consequences if my orders are not followed," the judge in my case was fond of saying. "If you don't think I will throw you in jail for disobeying court orders, just try me."

A judge is typically many things – educated, honest and well intentioned. A judge is also extremely arrogant – arrogant enough to believe that a little over-the-top theatrics, maybe a Jack Nicholson sneer or a Robert DeNiro delivery, will be enough to scare an alienating parent into obeying court orders designed to rebuild the child's relationship with the alienated parent.

However since the judge doesn't understand what motivates an alienating parent, he doesn't understand that his threats fall on deaf ears. The alienating parent believes he or she answers to a much higher authority – his or her God-given instincts that qualify the parent as the only person capable of acting in the child's best interests. An alienating parent isn't going to change his or her behavior just because a judge orders it – especially if he or she doesn't see the consequences.

Some judges do back up their tough talk with action. Newspapers, court records and the internet are increasingly telling stories about judges who take children away from the alienating parent and send them to live with the targeted parent. In one high-profile case, the judge took twin girls away from their alienating mother and sent them to live with their father. Later, an Appeals Court judge reversed the ruling and sent the children back to their mother. Ironically, the Appeals Court judge recognized the mother's unhealthy and damaging alienating behavior, but believed the children were better off with her anyway.

Some judges even send alienating parents to jail. In one example a judge sentenced a mother to 3 ½ years in prison for abduction, conspiracy and three counts of perjury. The mother fled Texas for Norfolk, Virginia and left the father wondering if his child was dead or alive. Then she lied in court about the child's whereabouts and falsely accused the father of sexual abuse. The judge's verdict exceeded the sentencing guidelines that recommended no more than six months behind bars. Why? The judge said the guidelines weren't the answer. Her honor said she was particularly upset that the mother falsely accused the father of sexually molesting their daughter and had lied repeatedly in court.

Around the same time, a judge in Wisconsin ordered a teenager against his will to enter counseling with his father and eventually visit him under the state's Juvenile in Need of Protection or Services (JIPS) law. The boy had said he was afraid of his father and had refused to visit him since he was 10. But the court ruled that there was no proof that the father sexually or physically abused the boy. Up until this case, the court only used the JIPS law to force runaways, habitual truants and dropouts to follow rules or face sanctions. Court officials said this was the first time the law was used in a case typically reserved for family court.

All judges have the ability to find the alienating parent in contempt of court. Monetary fines, a little jail time, and the very real danger that the judge will award final custody of the child to the formerly loved spouse might be enough to get him or her to stop the alienating behavior and obey any counseling and visitation orders. But the alienating parent is a quick study. Much as the alienated child learned he could do anything he wanted without consequences, the alienating parent learns the same lesson if the judge is unwilling to punish him or her for disobeying court orders.

Sadly, many judges don't punish the alienating parent for disobeying court orders aimed at addressing severe parental alienation. Remember that many judges consider alienation nothing more than bad parenting, and bad parenting is not a crime. They are also reluctant to impose any punishment on the parent that might cause the child any more pain. If a judge takes any money out of the alienating parent's pocket, that's money that the parent theoretically might have needed to support the child. If a judge throws the alienating parent in jail, even for a few hours, he runs the risk of further upsetting an emotionally troubled youngster already traumatized over the breakdown of his family. Award custody of the child to the alienated parent and remove the child from the only place the child considers "home?" Don't count on it. Judges rarely take such drastic measures.

Instead these judges often talk tough, issue orders without consequences, and continue the case until a later date -- all the while hoping that the parents will get tired of spending their money on attorney fees and reach an agreement before they're due back in court again. What these judges should do is take the time to understand parental alienation so they can recognize it in its earliest stages and intervene quickly. Otherwise, reaching the alienated child in time to restore the healthy relationship with the alienated parent is almost impossible.

* * * *

Ron Griffin: I can see you don't have a lot of respect for the court.

Mike: I have a great deal of respect for our judicial system. I have no respect for an individual who is entrusted to do the system's work and for a variety of self-serving or misguided reasons, allows every antiquated loophole and crack in the system to be exploited at the expense of parents and children.

Ron Griffin: You're obviously talking about the judge.

Mike: Yes.

Ron Griffin: I think you have to humanize the term "judge." A judge is nothing more than a person – a person who has voluntarily put him or herself in the position of making decisions that will affect other people's lives. Judges have a variety of backgrounds and a variety of experiences. Some judges are good; others are bad. Some judges have children; others don't. Some family court judges have never handled a divorce case. They know absolutely nothing about family law. Other judges were heavily involved in family practice before they made the bench. Judges are hundreds of thousands of people wearing robes. Some of these people know what they are doing and some don't.

Mike: That's not very comforting to anyone going to court looking for a legal resolution to a very personal problem.

Ron Griffin: The court system does not exist to fix problems. The court system exists as a last resort for people who failed to work things out on their own. Anytime a person puts a decision in a judge's hand, that person has to realize that sometimes the judge is going to be wrong.

Mike: As an attorney what do you do to ensure the judge reaches the right decision?

Ron Griffin: First of all, I can't predict how a judge will rule. If any attorney tells you he or she can predict how a judge will rule, that attorney is not telling the truth.

Having said that, knowing the judge is important. An attorney who practices in a particular community should be able to tell a client which judge will give the client a fair hearing and which judge will not.

An attorney should never waste time educating a judge about what the law is if the judge has been sitting on the bench for 20 years ruling on family cases. The judge has probably forgotten more about the law than the attorney will ever know. But when an attorney has a judge who doesn't know what's going on, the attorney has to spoon feed the judge information. The attorney shouldn't assume anything. He or she must be prepared to set out sufficient facts methodically and logically so the judge can reach the correct conclusion. This is particularly true in parental alienation cases.

First the attorney must tell the judge why he or she needs to make the ruling the attorney is asking the judge to make. Step two is for the attorney to build his or her case in increments. For example, an attorney building a case against an alienating parent shouldn't go into court on the first day of the case and ask the judge to take custody away from that parent. Finally, in a parental alienation case, or any custody case, the attorney must demonstrate the effect of the parent's negative behavior on the child. The attorney and client can bad-mouth the other parent all day long. But unless they can show that the alienating parent's conduct has had a detrimental effect on the child, it's a waste of time. Judges fully expect that each side is going to trash the other. That's the nature of divorce cases.

Mike: Theoretically, you make it sound so simple, sequential and logical. But practically, how often does the judge reach the right conclusion and take the necessary steps to protect the child from severe parental alienation? How often does a judge impose sanctions on an alienating parent for violating court orders related to the alienated parent and the child?

Ron Griffin: A judge rarely imposes sanctions on the alienating parent. Contempt of court is the knowing and willful violation of a court order. But there are no teeth in most court orders. A judge could order an alienating parent to pay a fine or the ex-spouse's legal fees, but is that really going to stop the alienating behavior? Probably not, and the judge will rarely impose harsher consequences, such as taking the child away from the alienating parent.

Mike: Why not?

Ron Griffin: Many judges, attorneys and psychologists believe removing the child from the alienating parent's home would destroy the child.

Mike: What happens if a psychologist testifies in court that a change in custody would be in the child's best interest?

Ron Griffin: The judge might agree to such a drastic course of action with enough expert testimony supporting that recommendation. The more evidence a judge has to hang his or her hat on, the better the chances. But unless a child has visible signs of physical or sexual abuse, a judge will usually take the middle ground with respect to custody and parenting time. Most judges are not tough enough to cut one parent out of the child's life – even when such drastic action is appropriate. They always err towards the middle ground –

issuing orders that keep a child with both parents –
even though for all practical purposes an alienating
parent and severely alienated child will render those
orders meaningless for the alienated parent.

Mike: So what's the answer?

Ron Griffin: There is no easy answer. A litigant can
always appeal a judge's decision. He or she might
get an Appeals Court to reverse a bad decision.
Judges don't like having their decisions reversed. If
a higher court reverses a judge's decisions enough
times, the judge will start paying attention. Judges
have their reputations to protect.

The real problem is not bad judges. The real
problem is that the adversarial system, our system,
of justice enhances parental alienation. This system
doesn't work for family law and contested custody
cases. The ongoing legal conflict is part of the
alienated child's problem.

Many practitioners believe a panel
consisting of a judge, a mental health professional,
and perhaps an education professional should rule
on contested custody cases. At the very least, the
legal system should be modified to include more
mental health professionals in the process. But
reform of this magnitude happens slowly. The only
thing we can do is keep pushing for reform and
legislation.

15

Solution

THE ORIGINAL TITLE TO THIS CHAPTER was *Solutions* – plural. But my journey through parental alienation led me to only one solution to a severely alienated child's entrenched and irreversible position. In order for a severely alienated child to rebuild his relationship with the alienated parent, the child must be removed from the alienating parent's sphere of influence. The child must live full-time with the alienated parent. He can't call, visit, or have any contact with the alienating parent – until the child is strong enough to withstand that parent's negative and destructive influence.

And the sound you just heard was many judges, attorneys and traditional family therapists gasping in indignation and disbelief.

Taking a severely alienated child away from the alienating parent is unfathomable to many child custody professionals. They believe such a radical course of action will somehow damage the child. Despite the fact that there is no clinical evidence to suggest that placing a severely alienated child with his or her one emotionally healthy parent will harm the child, most judges, attorneys and traditional mental health professionals would rather not rock the child's boat.

However, I did discover a process to rock the alienated child's boat and have the child benefit from the experience.

Reintegration – the process of helping a severely alienated child rebuild a relationship with his or her targeted parent – is being used by specialists working these very difficult cases. Specialists may be volunteers, medical doctors, psychologists, psychiatrists, social workers or therapists. In many cases it takes a combination of lay people and professionals to help a severely alienated child and parent begin rebuilding their relationship. While individual reintegration programs may vary, all programs typically focus on extensive physical contact – normal day-to-day contact – between the child and parent under the watchful eye of a trained facilitator. The program's goal is for the alienated child to rediscover a healthy, loving relationship with the alienated parent and eventually have loving relationships with both parents on his or her own terms.

"We take the view that alienated children aren't unhealthy," says Pamela Hoch, the founder of a non-profit agency specializing in rebuilding previously loving relationships between parents and children. "These children are just trying to survive as hostages in an alienation situation. We don't believe these children are sick. We take a more educational approach."

There are four elements to most programs. First the program facilitators must overcome the child's acting out and mistrust. Second, they focus on education rather than therapy. Then they help the child and parent rediscover good communication skills. Finally, they help the child build bridges to a new life that includes the formerly alienated parent, the parent's extended family and friends, and the alienating parent.

How does the reintegration process begin? The process begins in the courtroom. The judge gives the alienated parent full custody of the child and bans the alienating parent from having any contact with the child – until a solid bond exists between the child and the formerly alienated parent.

"No judge will take the necessary steps to address a severe case of parental alienation until a case is so bad that the child is completely alienated from the parent," says Dr. Mike Bone, another professional specializing in parent/child reintegration. "Many times I tell a parent, 'it must get worse before it can get better.' Usually the child will act out excessively about visiting the alienated parent. The child may send the most toxic hate mail imaginable to the parent. A judge usually must see that type of behavior before he or she will consider taking the necessary steps to successfully resolve the case."

Most reintegration specialists won't touch a case without the judge's full support and the court orders in place to back up that support. With court orders in hand, the specialist plans the child's transfer away from the alienating parent. A week or two before the transfer date, calls go out to the local sheriff's department, child welfare agency and even airport police if airline travel is involved. Hoch says a controlled environment during the transfer is essential on the practical, psychological and law enforcement levels. "All children refuse to go in the beginning. A severely alienated child will scream during a transfer, 'I'm being kidnapped, I'm being abducted,'" she says. "We must have strong, knowledgeable and trained people along the route to insure an orderly transfer to the parent's home, a rented facility or even a hotel room. Our goal is to get the child into the new environment as quickly as possible."

A compassionate, warm and strong position with the alienated child is also important to the success of the reintegration. During the transfer, a child often becomes physical. Even though most children understand that physical violence is unacceptable, the reintegration team sometimes needs the police to remind the child that hitting; punching and kicking won't be tolerated. "Once the child is removed from the environment where an alienating parent has influence, it is usually a relatively short period of time before the child calms down and the physical acting out stops," Bone says. "A severely alienated child generally knows he or she can only get away with inappropriate behavior with the alienating parent's support and when the behavior is directed at the alienated parent. Without the parents involved, the child typically calms down and behaves appropriately."

The alienated parent isn't usually involved in the transfer. This way, the child doesn't have the familiar target to direct his or her anger and bad behavior at. Instead, the child deals with a facilitator. A facilitator may be a mental health professional or may be someone working with a mental health professional. Typically, Hoch's organization uses someone older—a non-threatening grandfather or grandmother type – to explain to the child in very concrete, no-nonsense language, "This is happening, and there is nothing you can do about it. We know this is unpleasant for you, and we're here to help you get through it. But that doesn't mean it isn't going to happen or be any less unpleasant."

Naturally, the facilitator must overcome the child's mistrust. Hoch calls this period, "the cool-down" phase of the program. The cool-down phase could last anywhere from two hours to two weeks. During this part of the program the facilitator focuses on education rather than therapy. The facilitator informs the child in age-appropriate language what will happen next. Much like a project manager in a business meeting, the facilitator outlines the goals, objectives and parameters of the project – breaking down larger objectives into smaller, more manageable tasks.

"The facilitator is not the child's ally," Hoch explains. "This is an area where our approach differs from a traditional family therapist's approach." Many therapists believe that a child needs to feel as though the therapist is on the child's side in order to reintegrate the child with the alienated parent. We disagree. Our facilitator develops a relationship with the child – a relationship where the two may have different opinions – but a relationship where the facilitator is clearly in charge and calling the shots. A child wants structure. You wouldn't believe how safe the child feels with this approach."

While a facilitator doesn't have to be a trained mental health professional, an alienated parent probably wants a court-appointed counselor to supervise his or her reintegration case. This professional should stay in daily contact with the facilitator running the program. An alienated child needs a good long-term relationship with a therapist in order to address feelings and trauma that eventually come to the surface – sometimes years after the reintegration process.

The alienated parent may or may not have contact with the child during the cool-down period. However once the child calms down, the alienated parent is always in the picture. One big hurdle is breaking down the child's false beliefs about the alienated parent; i.e., the parent isn't the violent, dangerous and untrustworthy monster the child believes the parent to be. The facilitator and other volunteers accomplish this task through a series of age-appropriate reality checks. They lead the child and parent through simple, normal everyday activities. And the tasks are simple – getting dressed, doing laundry, making dinner, eating dinner together, cleaning up, going to movies, parks, and museums. The child and parent also get to watch each other interact with other people. This process benefits the parent as much as the child. Don't forget, in some cases the parent and child haven't been together in the same room for years. The parent often believes the child is the same child he or she knew before the alienation. That isn't the case.

While the child and parent are learning to trust each other again, the program is process driven. The facilitator is taking a firm position with both the parent and child in terms of the day's activities. But after a very short time – anywhere from a few hours to a few days – the parent and child start driving the process themselves. Driving the process involves more than the participants' deciding what they want to do, and when and where they want to do it. A parent/child-driven process does not wait for the facilitator to take the lead in communication, problem solving and decision-making. The parent and child initiate these discussions.

"In reality, no one can break down a child's false reality except the child. But by engaging the child and parent in normal activities, the child gets to see for him or herself that the parent doesn't fit the child's long-held beliefs. That's when the child's false belief system starts to crumble. When the child and parent start driving the process we know the reintegration has an excellent chance to succeed," Bone explains.

However, the parent and child's work is far from over. The two still haven't addressed the issues that led to their current relationship. In some cases, the parent and child could even live together and on the surface appear reintegrated – even though they're not. The two can't be fully reintegrated as long as one or both of them continues to sweep unresolved issues under a rug.

Bringing these issues out in the open is tricky. Negative comments about the alienating parent are strictly forbidden. Further, the parent may resist saying anything that could damage the new, fragile parent/child relationship. And the child may not feel safe saying anything. Enter the facilitator. The facilitator acts as a communication conduit between the parent and child. When the child starts questioning the differences between his or her distorted memory and his or her new reality, the child will typically broach the subject with the facilitator when the two are alone.

Ultimately, no one – not the facilitator, parent or anyone else – can change the child's mind about what did or didn't happen in the past. The only person who can do that is the child. And the only way the child can realize that his or her perception of the parent is wrong is to compare that perception with the reality in front of his or her eyes. "The child begins this process during the reintegration," Hoch explains. "But it could take the child as much as a year, long after the child and parent have left the intensive part of the program, for the child to open up to the parent about how he or she felt during the lost time. And finishing that conversation could take years. What we do is prepare the parent and child cognitively for the process."

Hoch's volunteers use storytelling, discussion exercises and meetings with other newly reintegrated families to equip the child and parent with the necessary tools to cope with their new relationship and prepare for the future. The key for the child and parent is discovering common ground, and very often the biological bond that exists between the child and parent is the best common ground. According to Hoch, even a child and parent who haven't seen each other for years still have common tastes, emotions and skills. "It's absolutely phenomenal to watch them rediscover all the areas they have in common," she says.

Even still, a successful reintegration does not guarantee a successful long-term relationship. The intensive part of the reintegration process usually lasts two to six weeks. A younger child who hasn't had any contact with the alienated parent in two or three years may need more time; a teenager who has already begun emotionally separating from his or her alienating parent may need less time. The key to long-term success is the child and parent's pre-alienation relationship. Were the two close? Did they have a healthy and strong bond? If the parent/child relationship was good, then their future looks bright.

However, even when the child and parent shared a healthy pre-alienation relationship their future could be complicated by something akin to a pendulum swinging back and forth. If the court allows a child to re-establish contact with the alienating parent too soon, the child begins swinging wildly between the two parents. According to Bone, the formerly alienated parent must remain calm during these swings and continue sending the child messages filled with love and support. The child's former facilitator could also step back into the child's life and help the child with his or her conflicted feelings.

Another key factor in the long-term success of the reintegration process is bridge relationships. For example, a child alienated from his or her mother may have stayed close to an aunt – the mother's sister. The aunt becomes the bridge relationship. Siblings also make excellent bridges. Bridge relationships are important because the "bridge" person has loving relationships with both the alienated child and parent. The bridge person provides a much-needed reality check for a reintegrated child experiencing the pendulum effect. These relationships become particularly important to the long-term success of the reintegration process once the formerly alienated child turns 18 years old and is beyond the court's jurisdiction. In an alienated family, a non-alienated child is often the key to restoring and maintaining the relationship between his alienated brother or sister and the parent.

* * *

Amanda Beck: We won't take your case.

Mike: I know. I'm just here to learn about your process. Where does it start?

Amanda Beck: Local family court judges generally preside over cases involving parental alienation. These judges rely very heavily on expert testimony and tend to be sensitive to local politics. Some are wonderful judges,

264

however most are very reluctant to take the necessary steps to realign the family structure so the child can re-establish a loving relationship with both parents.

Mike: I think the court-appointed psychologist in my case intellectually understood parental alienation, but his solution focused on the more traditional family therapy approach. The judge in my case refused to enforce his own orders. And to be fair, I didn't press for sole physical custody of my alienated son. I didn't want to destroy his relationship with his Mom. I just wanted a relationship with him too.

Amanda Beck: The most heartbreaking cases are the cases where the well-meaning counselor says, "The child needs the alienating parent." Our philosophy is the child needs both parents, but having both parents is not always best for the child. If the alienating parent were really pathological, we would recommend the child have no contact with this parent for a long, extended period of time. And this is where we get very unpopular with some mental health professionals, attorneys and judges. But the long-term results of reintegration are starting to show. I worked with children 15 years ago who are now adults. These kids turned into well-balanced, healthy, young men and women. Now they are establishing relationships with the alienating parents on their own terms.

Mike: Do you do therapy or counseling
                         with the child?

Amanda Beck: No. Court-ordered therapists
                         supervise our program, but most children, by
                         the time they get to us, have high anxiety
                         about meeting with a therapist. In addition,
                         we don't use the traditional therapist's,
                         "Let's work through this together so you
                         become used to it and happy" approach. The
                         truth is children will never be happy with the
                         fact that their parents divorced. Children
                         never get over the pain. Our goal is to help
                         the alienated child get on with his or her life
                         and become the person he or she was
                         destined to be before the child became
                         severely alienated from one parent.

Mike: What do you mean, be the person he or
                         she was destined to be?

Amanda Beck: We address two elements during the
                         reintegration process. The first element is
                         the reintegration of the child and parent. The
                         second element is reintegration of the child
                         within him or herself.

                         When a child is alienated from a
                         parent, the child is dispossessed from who
                         he or she is. The child's personality literally
                         disappears. Either the child takes on the
                         personality of the alienating parent or the
                         child becomes an actor – totally immersing
                         him or herself in a role. An alienated child
                         suppresses his or her own identity and our
                         program helps the child rediscover that
                         identity.

Mike: I don't understand something. Even though a child in your program rebuilds a healthy bond with the alienated parent, the child still has a strong, unhealthy emotional bond with the alienating parent. Does that bond ever break?

Amanda Beck: Sometimes the bond breaks and sometimes it doesn't. That's why the court's orders forbidding any contact with the severely alienating parent are so important. We've found that the children who grow up to be the emotionally healthiest adults are those children who have no contact with their severely alienating parents. When these children become young adults they're mentally and emotionally capable of initiating a relationship with the alienating parents on their own terms.

Mike: What do you mean, their own terms?

Amanda Beck: When alienated children reach out to their alienating parents as young adults they have a lot of conflicting feelings. Children want parents they can be proud of. A formerly alienated child must come to terms with the alienating parent's unhealthy, black-and-white view of the world and bury any idealism he or she may have had about the parent. The formerly alienated child must reach a point where he or she says, 'I love Mom/Dad – warts and all.'

Mike: Does a severely alienated child ever try faking his or her way through the reintegration process? I can imagine a child going along with the program with the ultimate goal of getting out of your controlled environment and back to the alienating parent?

Amanda Beck: Happens all the time – especially with older children.

I call the child who tries to fake his or her way through the program 'the manipulative child.' The manipulative child's goal is to return to the alienating parent. But the reintegration process really undermines the child's position. Don't forget, the child is living with the alienated parent – either in the parent's home, a rented facility or even a hotel room during the early stages of the program. The child inevitably starts having a good time and rediscovering the normal, healthy relationship he or she shared with the parent before the alienation. The child may arrive with plans to put something over on us, but he or she leaves reintegrated.

The child who presents the bigger challenge for us is the child who goes into emotional lockdown. This child becomes completely robotic. He or she will shut out other people. On the surface this child may be polite and even cooperative, but underneath the surface the child is emotionally committed to, and entrenched in, his or her alienated position.

Without exception, the children who fake it or go into lockdown are the children

268

who know that the reintegration program has an end date. In these cases a well-intentioned judge ordered the child to spend a fixed period of time with the alienated parent with the understanding that the child would resume a relationship with the alienating parent. You can't have a successful reintegration and an end date. Our courts just don't know this yet.

Mike: How do you discipline the child who doesn't listen or follow the rules?

Amanda Beck: When you have a severely alienated child, very often the child's sense of boundaries and sense of discipline has been completely distorted. The rules a parent would impose on a normal child won't work with an alienated child. I strongly disagree with people who say 'tough love works.' Tough love works occasionally. But I have found that if we try normal discipline with an alienated child, the child continues believing that the alienated parent is a big monster. The child's sense of right and wrong is totally distorted.

Instead we use a subtle form of discipline. We call it, Need-Centered Discipline. We impose discipline on the child though the child's physical needs. For example, in the beginning an alienated child will never sit down at the table for a meal with the parent. When that happens we tell the child, 'Okay, but if you don't sit down at the table you don't get any dinner. But feel free to help yourself to something from the

269

refrigerator later on.' The child will usually grab some peanut butter crackers or something equally unappealing and go to bed hungry. The child can't complain because skipping dinner at the table was his or her decision. But after a day or two of eating peanut butter crackers the child decides that dinner at the table isn't so bad. We impose our structure on the child, but very subtly.

Mike: It sounds to me that your methods would be very effective with younger children, but not teenagers.

Amanda Beck: We've had some of our best success with teenagers. Older children are more cognitively developed. They can separate their needs from their emotions. Older children are also separating emotionally from their parents.

Mike: Well, thank you for your time. I should be going.

Amanda Beck: I'm sorry we can't help you. In your case you'll have to wait until your younger child moves out of his alienating mother's sphere of influence before you two can have a relationship again. Going away to college is a big breakthrough time for many alienated children and parents. At that point your older son would be able to act as the bridge relationship without fear of retribution from his mother. If he maintains a relationship with his brother, he can facilitate a breakthrough for you.

16

Coping

MOVE ON EMOTIONALLY. Don't concentrate on the relationship you once had with the alienated child. Get past the anger. Don't beat yourself up. Focus on the positive. Understand how you got here. Keep your negative emotions in a box and don't let them out too often. Recite the serenity prayer: *God grant me the serenity to accept the things I cannot change, courage to change the things I cannot accept and the wisdom to know the difference.*

Alienated parents have heard it all. And most alienated parents have just one question for all the professionals and well-meaning people who offer such wonderful advice: "How? And while you're at it, could you possibly provide a road map, instruction booklet or assembly manual?" Just keep in mind that alienated parents are forced to deal with all sorts of realities such as:

- Rush hour traffic. The longer the commute, the more time there is to think about the alienated child and get upset, depressed or angry.

- Airports. The overcrowded plane with its too small seats looks pretty good after watching parents and children of all ages engaged in tearful goodbyes and happy reunions.

- Movies. Mel Gibson single handedly defeats the British in his revolutionary war epic but his daughter won't talk to him because she feels Gibson's character abandoned her. Ouch – that musket shot found its mark. Or Tom Hanks as a cold hit man who bonds with his older son when he isn't killing people. Double ouch – that boy wants to be with his father even though Dad kills people for a living. Then there is Will Smith and his real-life son playing a homeless father and son living in public bathrooms. Their real life bond comes right through the screen. Thousands of parent/child scenes play out on movie and television screens every night. These scenes mentally and emotionally transport alienated parents back to the relationships they once shared with their children, and remind them that those relationships don't exist anymore.

- Music. Songs of lost love and regret in every format on every station, in elevators, malls, dentists' offices and when someone on the other end of the phone says, "Please hold on." The most painful songs for an alienated parent are songs about children. Have you listened to Harry Chapin's *Cats in the Cradle,* Don Henley's *The End of the Innocence,* Eric Clapton's *Tears in Heaven or* Will Smith's *Just the Two of Us? Cats in the Cradle* and *The End of the Innocence* rate a ten on any alienated parent's Guilt-o-Meter. *Tears in Heaven* and *Just the Two of Us* are a three-tissue cry-a-long for an alienated parent.

- Birthdays. Boy and Girl Scout outings. Recitals. Graduations. Picnics. Soccer games. Restaurants. Grocery shopping. Back-to-School sales. You name the experience and any alienated parent can give you an example of the emotions leaving the box, the anger rising to the surface, and all the excellent coping suggestions instantly becoming useless. The overwhelming loss and pain that come with losing a child to parental alienation combined with the lack of closure is a powerful and emotionally destructive combination. It's easy to slide back into denial. It's even easier to get angry again. So how do alienated parents get past the loss of a relationship that they feel was wrongfully stolen away? How do they get past knowing that their children are growing up in an emotionally destructive environment, and there isn't anything they can do about it? How do they deal with innocent daily events that serve as painful reminders of what they don't have anymore?

* * * *

Dr. Davies: Hello Mike.

Mike: Is it time for our next session already?

Dr. Davies: No, but you're getting carried away. You need to calm down.

Mike: You think I'm letting my emotions get the better of me?

Dr. Davies: Perhaps a little bit. Take a deep breath and I'll answer your questions.

It's true that an alienated parent must deal with a loss that he or she feels was wrongfully stolen away. Unfortunately, the loss stays with the parent as long as the parent is separated from the child. The parent's goal shouldn't just be restoring the relationship, but also coping with the loss.

273

The best coping tool is understanding the subject matter intellectually. When an alienated parent understands parental alienation, that understanding provides the parent with an emotional anchor. The alienated parent sees that alienation is not about what kind of mother or father you are. Rather, alienation is about your ex-spouse's struggles with unresolved abandonment issues.

Religion is another coping mechanism. Many alienated parents turn to their churches or synagogues and find great comfort in faith and prayer. Historically, people have always drawn strength from their religious beliefs during difficult times. I would, however, caution alienated parents about relying too much on prayer for a positive outcome to their situations. Prayer may ultimately bring alienated children and parents together again, but the reunion may not happen within a time-frame that seems acceptable or fair to alienated parents. Remember, alienated parents must cope with the loss as well as try to rebuild the previously loving relationships.

Receiving validation or public acknowledgement also helps an alienated parent deal with the injustice of his or her situation. Anyone who really knows the kind of parent the alienated parent is can offer the validation. Obviously, validation from a professional with experience in parental alienation cases is even better. The professional is emotionally detached from the parent's situation and looks at it objectively. Getting this type of support is a very important part of the parent's recovery process.

On many different levels, healthy distractions prevent the alienated parent from obsessing over a situation over which he or she has no control. Physical outlets allow the parent to reduce the stress and tension that people tend to carry around during difficult times. Writing in a journal or diary helps the parent offload the emotional impact of his or her situation. And don't forget social or recreational activities and volunteer work. Just because parental alienation exists in the parent's life doesn't mean the parent can't ever have fun or do something rewarding.

One thing I would caution any parent against is dwelling continuously on the negative aspects of the situation. The occasional pity party is fine, but a parent shouldn't dwell on the situation so much that the parent's negative frame of mind becomes self-perpetuating.

Dwelling on the negative is a problem for many alienated parents because they feel shame over their inability to protect their children and their reputations. But an alienated parent shouldn't feel ashamed. The parent didn't do anything wrong. In fact, most alienated parents should feel very proud of their efforts to protect their children. Many parents have devoted years, not to mention all their financial resources and a large piece of their emotional health, to exploring options that could potentially help their children.

Mike: Okay, how about my second question? How does an alienated parent get past knowing that the child is growing up in an emotionally destructive environment, and there isn't anything he or she can do about it?

275

Dr. Davies: In spite of the campaign of denigration against the alienated parent, the home environment of the alienating parent and child is often relatively healthy. The alienating parent does love and take care of the child. On the surface, all the child's needs are met. However beneath the surface the alienating parent has taught the child some very damaging lessons.

An alienated child doesn't know how to address and resolve anger and mend relationships. The child also believes that there are no consequences for inappropriate behavior. These lessons will stay with the child for a very long time – probably until the child is separated from the alienated parent. At that point the individual will have the emotional freedom to develop healthier attitudes about anger, resolving conflict and forgiveness.

Mike: How does an alienated parent deal with innocent daily events that serve as painful reminders of what they don't have anymore?

Dr. Davies: There is nothing that can prepare alienated parents from missing developmental milestones such as the first pair of shoes, first haircut or first day of school. Those days would be difficult for anyone who has lost a child. Alienated parents should remember that there is no correlation between being a good parent and being an alienated parent.

On a daily basis, alienated parents must know their limits regarding their abilities to deal with events that serve as painful reminders of relationships that no longer exist. Talking to other people about these feelings is a very important way of letting go and moving forward. Feelings acknowledged ultimately disappear. Feelings denied often result in little to no change. Alienated parents must also acknowledge that acceptance is a process that takes time and effort.

17

Epilogue

April 15, 2006

I'M 46 YEARS OLD AND I'M still dreaming. However my old dreams about Adam have been replaced with newer dreams that more accurately reflect the current state of our relationship.

These days I dream my 13-year-old son walks up to me with a smile on his face. I tell Adam I love him. He says, "I love you too." I say, "I miss you." In response Adam says, "I miss you too." In my dream I'm afraid to ask the next question. "Would you like to get together and do something," I finally ask? "Okay," he says with the smile still firmly planted on his face. Then I wake up and face the reality of being an alienated parent – no smile, no get-together and no Adam.

In my dreams I see Adam the way he looked the last time I saw him up close – June 2005. Adam graduated from middle school that night. Beth and Adam, with a big assist from yours truly, celebrated by having me arrested.

Adam didn't want me attending his graduation banquet. I showed up anyway. I walked over to the table where he and Beth were sitting, congratulated the graduate, and moved to a table on the other side of the room. Adam never said a word.

After about five minutes Adam got up from his table and walked outside. Beth followed him. After another ten minutes I decided to leave. I made my point – Adam knew I cared enough to show up. If he saw me leave maybe he would come back inside and enjoy his graduation ceremonies.

As I approached my car I saw Adam doing something to the passenger side door. I yelled at him to get away from the car. He took off running. I took off after him and demanded to know what he did to my car. Later I noticed that he had scratched the car door with a key or coin but I didn't know that at the time. Adam refused to answer me. He just punched me. At that point Beth, who had watched the entire scene unfold, ran up and screamed for someone to call the police. She was more interested in having me arrested than addressing Adam's vandalism and disgusting behavior. I later figured out why.

The judge had issued his ruling earlier that day, and not only did the judge rule against Beth's custody request, but he also didn't give her the financial settlement she wanted. However, because of a clerical mistake at the courthouse, I wouldn't know any of this for another week. While I was oblivious to my newly divorced status, Beth knew about it and must not have been happy with the outcome. When I called her, "an alienating psychopath," I gave her yet another stick to hit me with. She called the police and told them I was "harassing her."

The police took statements from everyone. Eight days later an officer left me a message on my home phone. He wanted me to come to the police station. I was being arrested. The charge was Breach of Peace.

The charge was eventually dropped, but not before Beth had the court issue a protective order against me on Adam's behalf. I wasn't allowed to have any contact with my son for two months – no court-ordered therapy sessions, phone calls, emails or letters. I resumed my attempts to communicate with Adam after the protective order was lifted; but I had about as much success after the order was lifted as I had before the order. Adam always hung up on me and rarely responded to my invitations, gifts and emails. When he did respond, his messages were full of anger, hate and loathing.

While the protective order was still in place, Beth took Adam to the hospital emergency room. Allegedly, he threatened to kill himself again. Beth called me and said I should meet her at the hospital. "No way, not unless you remove the protective order," I said. She tried telling me that she didn't know anything about a protective order. I knew better. The only reason Beth wanted me at the hospital was so she could have me arrested again. I wouldn't budge. When Adam refused to talk to the emergency room doctors, the doctors sent him and Beth home.

The court-ordered therapist, Dr. Harris, was still marginally involved with Adam at that point. He met with Adam once or twice more after our last session in May 2005. Harris reported that Adam didn't behave any better when they were alone than when I was there. After Adam's latest suicide threat, Harris asked Beth and me to meet with him. I agreed. After all, what did I have to lose?

Harris told both of us what I already knew – Adam was an extremely troubled child. He hammered away at Beth to hold Adam accountable for his actions. For her part, Beth hung on the psychologist's every word like Harris was sharing the secret to eternal life. She enthusiastically agreed that Adam needed his father in his life. Beth put on quite a convincing performance. She seemed so genuinely interested in repairing my relationship with Adam as a way to help our child that I even believed she was sincere – for about two seconds. That day in September 2005 was the last time Harris ever saw Beth. He never saw Adam again either.

In the meantime, the court appearances dragged on. The judge kept the case open to monitor Adam's progress in therapy. The only problem was Beth wasn't taking Adam to therapy. The judge would hear this and threaten serious consequences if his orders weren't followed. But rather than find Beth in contempt of court for not taking take Adam to therapy, his honor would pass on my ever-present contempt motion, make a long-winded threat or two, set a date for another status conference, and send everyone on their respective ways. We had all sat through this performance so many times we were like an audience at the *Rocky Horror Picture Show*. We could repeat the words along with the judge. Beth knew he would never back up his tough talk with any action. She left the courtroom after each lecture without giving the judge's tired, old performance another thought. We returned to the courthouse for months before the judge, despite my protests, admitted defeat and rescinded all Adam's therapy orders.

In the second half of 2005 Jared had own his problems with Beth. One night in August I received a call from the local police department. Beth called the police because Jared refused to get rid of some exercise equipment I gave him. The officer asked me who owned the equipment. I said Jared. I don't know what Beth expected the police to do about the situation. All I know is Jared spent the weekend with me, and when he returned to the house on Monday the equipment was gone.

A few months later Jared called me from Beth's house at 2:00 a.m. He was very upset and demanded I come pick him up immediately. I kept asking what was wrong and he would only say, "Just come get me." When I arrived at the house Jared was waiting outside with two big plastic bags containing his most prized possessions. Beth had thrown her son out of the house. His crime? In response to the Material Girl's demand that Jared bring clothes I bought him to her house so she wouldn't have to buy him clothes, Jared responded, "Why don't you use your child support to buy me clothes?"

Lately Jared and Beth have reached an uneasy truce. Jared continues to split his time between the two households. He's even developed a sense of humor, albeit a sarcastic sense of humor, about his relationship with his Mom. If you go to Jared's web site, you can read his journal. Under the heading, *Fun with Divorce,* Jared writes about an exchange he allegedly had with Beth:

- Beth: Jared, if you say one more word, I'm calling your father and you're going to go live with him."

- Jared: I've got $370 a week in child support that says different.

- Beth: (Speechless)

Sarcastic and inappropriate? Yes. Bad numbers? Definitely. However, what Jared lacked in diplomacy and accuracy he makes up for in truthfulness. Jared knows he can continue living in Beth's house as long as I'm paying child support for him.

All in all, I think Jared has come through this ordeal relatively unscathed and well adjusted. He is very much aware of his second-class citizenship in Beth's house and just accepts his status as a trade-off for maintaining a healthy relationship with me. In the final analysis, Jared loves his Mom the way he should – unconditionally. He floats back and forth between the households balancing schoolwork, a part-time job, extra-curricular activities and an active social life. He doesn't really share with me any details of his day-to-day life with his Mom and brother, and that's the way it should be. I do my best to respect his privacy, even though Jared remains my only window into Adam's life. Every now and then my need to hear something, anything, about my other son overwhelms me. I ask Jared to, "Throw me a bone. Tell me something." Sometimes he does and sometimes he doesn't. Right now my biggest problem with Jared is the same problem thousands of parents are facing with children Jared's age – getting our high school students to start focusing on college.

Without the court's spotlight shining on her anymore, Beth doesn't even pretend to act in her children's best interests if she thinks there's even the slightest chance that I might benefit too. She always keeps her telephone answering machine on and never returns my calls or gives Jared my messages. Beth also refuses to let Jared sleep at her house on days that are technically "my days." As a result, I've missed more than one out-of-town business meeting. If I can't reschedule a business trip or make arrangements for Jared to stay with a friend, he sometimes comes with me. Jared has probably seen the concierge level of more hotels than most of his peers.

Beth cooperates even less on anything concerning Adam. She doesn't give me copies of Adam's report cards, school picture order forms or Back-to-School Night notices. I don't even know when Adam is sick until the insurance company's Explanation of Benefits shows up in my mailbox and indicates Adam went to the doctor.

Sadly, my relationship with Adam remains the same. He refuses every invitation I make, hangs up the phone if I try and talk to him, and doesn't acknowledge my gifts or respond to most of my emails and instant messages. He doesn't speak, see or respond to his grandparents, aunts, uncles and cousins either. To the best of my knowledge, Adam hasn't seen the inside of a therapist's office, any therapist's office, since the day Dr. Harris told Beth and me that Adam is an extremely troubled child. In the meantime, his grades have plummeted, Jared tells me Adam has few friends, and from what I can determine my youngest child spends most of his free time alone playing games on his computer.

These days Adam uses the "block" feature on his electronic mail system to prevent any message from my screen name from reaching him. Thankfully, any combination of letters and numbers make up a new, valid screen name and there are an infinite number of potential screen names in cyberspace. For every screen name he blocks, I create a new one. Sometimes when I send him a message under a newly created screen name I can even engage him in a line or two of "Guess who this is?" Of course, he figures out who I am quickly and then he doesn't respond anymore. Sometimes he even logs off. But at least I have time to tell him I love him and miss him before he goes off to block my new screen name. Every time I get through I consider it a victory. Not only do I get past Beth and Adam's defenses; I also let my alienated child know I haven't forgotten him. Small victories are better than no victories.

I once believed that when Beth got involved in another relationship she might release her grip on Adam a little bit. Well, she did find a new relationship just a few months after I moved out. Her new boyfriend met the boys and slept at the house even before the divorce was final. Beth and her friend are still together; yet her grip on Adam's emotions remains as strong as ever. Clearly, I was wrong about the effect a new relationship would have on both Beth and Adam. Today I believe that Beth could hit the lottery in the morning, discover a cure for cancer in the afternoon, and have the most romantic experience of her life in the evening. Yet at the end of the day she would still have enough anger inside to tell Adam that, "Your father abandoned us. Your father abused us. Your father doesn't deserve your love or attention."

A few months ago a woman who works in my office and who knows about my alienated parent status told me about her husband. He hadn't spoken to his four children in 30 years. More precisely, his children wouldn't talk to him since he left their mother. This man had grandchildren he didn't even know existed. Years before Dr. Richard Gardner uttered the phrase, "parental

285

alienation," my co-worker's husband was a classic case of a severely alienated father.

Earlier this year one daughter called him, than a second daughter called, and finally a third daughter picked up the phone. The fourth daughter is still holding out. Today this father considers himself the luckiest man on the face of the earth. He has a wonderful relationship with three of his children and all of his grandchildren.

I still find it hard to believe that I lost an 11-year-old child and may not get him back until he has children of his own – if then. I still want to believe we'll play catch using the new baseball glove Adam gave me for Father's Day in 2004. Maybe I'll play catch with Adam again, and maybe I won't. Much like the Dad who considers himself the luckiest man on earth to have a relationship with his daughters after 30 years, one common element bonds all alienated parents together. We love our alienated children unconditionally. Our lives, our hearts and our doors are always open to them. Even after 30 years. We just hope they don't take that long to come around.

18

Epilogue II

REMEMBER THAT UNEASY TRUCE between Jared and Beth? I should have found a better way to describe Jared's relationship with his Mom. An analogy to a volcano that could potentially erupt at any time would have been more accurate. Last night the volcano erupted.

Beth threw her son out of the house – again. This time it appears Jared has no intention of going back. Unlike last time, when Jared left Beth's house with things he probably just wanted to take over to our place anyway, this time he cleaned out his room. My car was packed.

The precipitating event had something to do with Jared and Adam's dead pet ferret and the appropriate burial place for the deceased in Beth's back yard. The ferret died while Jared and I were away. According to Jared, Beth said they would bury the ferret when he came back. So when Jared got home from school yesterday he dug a hole in Beth's back yard. Beth wasn't home. When Beth saw the hole she erupted.

I'm pretty sure Beth's reaction had less to do with a hole in her back yard and more to do with the fact that Jared and I spent the previous ten days together – including his birthday and Thanksgiving – in Florida. Beth still seethes over her inability to disrupt my relationship with Jared. The thought of us enjoying ourselves over such a long period of time probably ate away at her the entire time we were away. I imagine her anger built with each passing day. When she finally had Jared back at her house, she exploded.

Beth insisted that Jared wait in the garage until I arrived to pick him up. The only trouble was, I was out of the office and my cell phone was turned off. Neither one of them could reach me. Except for the time he spent packing up his room, Jared sat in the garage for two hours.

On my way over I called and tried talking to Jared. Naturally, Beth wouldn't let me talk to him. One time Jared picked up the phone, and Beth did the same thing she used to do when I tried talking to Adam – she listened to every word and screamed in the background. Jared yelled at her more than he talked to me. The language Beth and Jared directed at each other contained every imaginable profanity in endless creative combinations. However when Jared screamed, "You treat me like shit!" I heard the pain in his voice. I also heard in his voice that he was finished allowing Beth to take her never-ending supply of anger out on him for the simple crime of loving his Dad.

And where was Adam the entire time? Jared reported that when Beth removed Jared's television set from his room so Jared couldn't take it with him, Adam jumped Jared from behind in order to create a clear path for his Mom. Jared once told me that even though Adam united with Beth against me, Jared believed Adam would always, "have my back." Sadly, Jared learned that "having the alienating parent's back" is a full-time job for a severely alienated child. In the child's mind, anyone who angers the parent angers the child – even if that person happens to be his brother.

19

The Final Entry

May 20, 2007

I'M PUSHING 50 YEARS OLD and yes, I'm still dreaming.

Sadly, my dreams are still the only place where Adam lets me into his life. I don't dream about Adam as frequently as I once did, but when I do he is still 11 years old and happy to see me. In one dream I said to Adam, "This isn't real. We're dreaming, right?" Adam smiled and nodded his head yes. Then I woke up. I wasn't sad or upset. I just rolled over and went back to sleep. It's been almost three years.

I still reach out to Adam with the occasional email, card, invitation and small gift. However over time Adam became much better at blocking emails, so I can only write to his old childhood screen name that exists under my account. The only way Adam can ignore my notes to that account is by refusing to log in – and that is exactly what he does.

I stopped calling Adam earlier this year. One Friday night I walked into the pizza place where Beth and I used to eat with the kids when we were married. Beth, her boyfriend (now fiancé), and a couple of other people were eating dinner. Adam wasn't with them. I called Adam at Beth's house and asked how come he passed up dinner at one of his favorite restaurants. He hung up. I waited a few minutes and called back. When he picked up the phone I asked, "Why can't you answer a simple question?"

In response Adam asked me to stop calling him. He didn't yell. He didn't curse. He didn't threaten to call the police or beat me up. He simply asked, softly and with a tired resignation in his voice that I've come to know well. Adam even said "please."

In that moment I recognized a young man who is painted into a corner and just trying to survive his painful situation. I haven't called back. If Adam's life is easier without the sound of my voice reminding him that our estrangement isn't my choice, then that's the least I can do. I'll leave him alone secure in the knowledge that he knows I love him, miss him, and the door to my life is always open to him.

Acknowledgements

I ALWAYS BELIEVED THAT WRITING a book was a lonely and solitary effort. I was wrong. Many people contributed to *A Family's Heartbreak: A Parent's Introduction to Parental Alienation* in one way or another. I just wish I could completely identify everyone and give them the recognition they deserve.

Let's start with my collaborator, Dr. Joel Davies. Our "sessions," mostly over breakfast or lunch, were both an education in parental alienation and free therapy. Joel helped me write this book and deal with my status as an alienated parent. The fact that you are reading these words is proof of his skills in both areas.

I'd also like to thank Joel's partner Scott. I invaded Scott's business and home. Scott delivered drafts of the book to Joel and returned Joel's scribbled notes to me. His good humor and friendship eased the guilt that I felt over invading his life.

While Ron Griffin and Amanda Beck are fictional characters, the professionals who shared the expertise that Ron and Amanda shared with me are not. So I'd also like to thank Attorney Gary Israel, Attorney Bonnie Amendola, Dr. Randy Rand, Dr. Mike Bone, Dr. Richard Warshak and Pamela Hoch for their contributions and insights. In addition, I would like to thank Dr. Jayne A. Major, Dr. Douglas Darnell, Dr. Mike Walsh and the family of Dr. Richard Gardner for allowing me to quote so extensively from their work.

I would also like to thank literary agent Jack Scovil for sharing his experience and insights to help a first-time author navigate the ups and downs of the publishing world.

Kurt Gibson from Inergy Group in Wilton, Connecticut also deserves a heartfelt thank you. I'm a writer, not a graphic designer, so I am eternally grateful that a graphic designer with Kurt's expertise took an interest in this project and helped me with the design elements, website and printing process.

Many people reviewed the manuscript at one point or another and they all have my thanks. Three former colleagues in particular deserve special recognition.

Karen Armour's edits and suggestions would have put the best editor at the most prestigious publishing house to shame. Mary Flieller encouraged me to tell my story and keep the book's format whenever I was ready to start over. Finally, Liz Brummond's assistance and friendship were invaluable during the writing, publishing, web design and marketing process.

I've often said that I would have had to write this book from a psychiatric ward if it weren't for the love and support of my family and friends during my darkest days as an alienated parent. The truth is I wouldn't have been able to write my name if it weren't for them.

Thank you to my parents for their unconditional love, unwavering support and supreme confidence in my abilities as both a writer and a Dad. I've been fortunate to have both my parents in my life for every single day of my life and I'm a better person for their involvement.

Thanks too, to my sister and her husband; and my brother and his wife. Knowing they were standing by if I needed anything was like knowing where I could anchor a boat in rough seas.

I am fortunate to have friends who are like family and family who are like friends. They all helped me stay sane while I lived through the insanity that is parental alienation. I would be remiss if I didn't recognize Lee and Donna, Barbara and Bob, Jeff and Joannie, Mark H. and Mark K. for their love, support and patience. Yes, patience. They've been listening to me talk about parental alienation and this book for years. When they got tired of listening to me they were kind enough not to mention it.

My son Jared deserves a very special and heartfelt thank you. Jared was the child who refused to be alienated. I know Jared paid a heavy price for his neutrality, and I admire him for his strength, convictions and willingness to speak out as a child of divorce. During an interview the reporter asked Jared, "What's the hardest part about having a relationship with your Dad when your brother refuses to have anything to do with him?" Jared responded, "I feel like I have to be both sons." I hope Jared knows that I only want him to be himself. Any parent would be lucky to have a son like Jared in his or her life.

My wife Kelly is an incredible woman. From day one she bore the brunt of my anger, pain, depression, helplessness and frustration – over and over again. I'm certain I wouldn't have had the strength to write this book if it wasn't for her constant love, support and encouragement. I've been writing professionally for almost 30 years, and in all that time I haven't yet come across words that can adequately express my love and admiration for Kelly. I am truly blessed to have her in my life.

Finally, I want to thank one very special young man and three beautiful young ladies.

I can't image many things more painful than being rejected by a child you love; so when other children show you they love you and miss you – that's the best medicine to heal an alienated parent's damaged soul. My nephew Michael and my nieces Lisa, Kylee and Alyssa constantly remind me that not all children believe I am unworthy of their love and attention. I'll always be grateful for that. I look forward to staying close to them for many years to come.

Mike Jeffries
February 2007